Richard Clapton is a much-loved legend of Australian music, the performer and songwriter of many iconic Australian hit songs: 'Deep Water', 'The Best Years of Our Lives', 'Goodbye Tiger', 'Glory Road', 'Lucky Country', 'I Am an Island', 'Trust Somebody', 'Capricorn Dancer' and 'Girls on the Avenue'.

As a producer Richard worked on the second INXS album, *Underneath the Colours* (1981), which included the first two hit singles that launched the band's rise to international fame. To date he has released nineteen albums, many of which have achieved gold or platinum status.

Australian rock music historian Ian McFarlane has described Clapton as 'one of the most important Australian songwriters'. On 12 October 1999, Clapton was inducted into the Australian Recording Industry Association (ARIA) Hall of Fame. In 2014 he celebrates 40 years in the music industry.

www.richardclapton.com

THE BEST YEARS OF OUR LIVES

Richard Clapton

SYDNEY·MELBOURNE·AUCKLAND·LONDON

This book is dedicated to my daughters, Montana and Saskia.

All attempts have been made to trace and acknowledge the owners of copyright material.
If you have any information in that regard, please contact the publisher at the address below.

Photography credits
Author's collection: pages 1, 15, 31, 45, 59, 73, 85, 93, 123, 137, 147, 159, 177, 219 and 245;
Tim Bauer: pages 209 and 279; Patrick Jones Studio: page 267; Bob King: page 167;
Wendy McDougall: page 305; Philip Morris: page 105; Philip Mortlock: pages 191 and 231;
Marcus Tomlinson: page 293; and Graeme Webber: page 257.

First published in 2014

Copyright © Richard Clapton 2014

All rights reserved. No part of this book may be reproduced or transmitted in
any form or by any means, electronic or mechanical, including photocopying,
recording or by any information storage and retrieval system, without prior
permission in writing from the publisher. The Australian *Copyright Act 1968*
(the Act) allows a maximum of one chapter or 10 per cent of this book, whichever
is the greater, to be photocopied by any educational institution for its educational
purposes provided that the educational institution (or body that administers it) has
given a remuneration notice to Copyright Agency (Australia) under the Act.

Allen & Unwin
83 Alexander Street
Crows Nest NSW 2065
Australia
Phone: (61 2) 8425 0100
Email: info@allenandunwin.com
Web: www.allenandunwin.com

Cataloguing-in-Publication details are available
from the National Library of Australia
www.trove.nla.gov.au

ISBN 978 1 76011 059 8

Internal design by Darian Causby

Set in 12.5/20pt Chapparal Pro by Post Pre-press Group, Australia

Printed and bound in Australia by Griffin Press

10 9 8 7 6 5 4 3 2 1

The paper in this book is FSC certified.
FSC promotes environmentally responsible,
socially beneficial and economically viable
management of the world's forests.

Contents

1 ❖ Lucky Country ❖ 1

2 ❖ I Wanna Be a Survivor ❖ 15

3 ❖ Burn Down Your Bridges ❖ 31

4 ❖ Southern Germany ❖ 45

5 ❖ Prussian Blue ❖ 59

6 ❖ Down the Road ❖ 73

7 ❖ Last Train to Marseilles ❖ 85

8 ❖ Girls on the Avenue ❖ 93

9 ❖ Need a Visionary ❖ 105

10 ❖ Goodbye Tiger ❖ 123

11 ❖ Deep Water ❖ 137

12 ❖ Out on the Edge Again ❖ 147

13 ❖ Hearts on the Nightline ❖ 159

14 ❖ Ace of Hearts ❖ 167

15 ❖ Dark Spaces ❖ 177

16 ❖ I Am an Island ❖ 191

17 ❖ The Best Years of Our Lives ❖ 209

18 ❖ Katy's Leaving Babylon ❖ 219

19 ❖ Solidarity ❖ 231

20 ❖ Glory Road ❖ 245

21 ❖ Distant Thunder ❖ 257

22 ❖ The Underground ❖ 267

23 ❖ Emperor's New Clothes ❖ 279

24 ❖ Up Where the Angels Fly ❖ 293

25 ❖ Here Inside of Me ❖ 305

You don't know what you've got til it's gone ❖ 316

Discography ❖ 329

Index of songs ❖ 337

1

'Standing on the corner,
with the sunlight in my eyes'

Lucky Country

It was 1966 and Sydney was bathed in the brilliance of summer. Black and white television had only been introduced to the suburban masses a few years earlier and, as I recall, when I was a little kid, programs like *Leave It to Beaver* and *Father Knows Best* were already designing a rough sketch which would fast become the tapestry of our lives in much the same way as *The Kardashians* and other gaudy plastic TV soaps have become the blueprint of the current generation of Australians.

I grew up with the *Leave It to Beaver* generation. Beaver Cleaver's family would have been a mighty fine role model if only they and the world they lived in had been real. Alas this was not the case, so the rather gawky Australian attempts to emulate these TV fantasies only resulted in a homogenised culture that didn't even belong to us.

As for cutting edge music, Australia in the sixties was a bit of a wasteland. The only incident of note during my school years that had real impact on my music career was spending a day with the Rolling Stones in 1965, when I was in my late teens. A kid called Ross was my best friend at school and figured prominently in my life during the sixties. We had another friend at school, David, who had been forced to leave school early—I think his single mother could no longer afford the fees. Anyway, David went to work for Movietone News, the newsreel company, which we thought was fantastic. What a job! All that money and independence and an elite gig with the media as well.

The Rolling Stones had long been established as our demigods. At school, because Ross and my other friends were 'day boys', they would buy me the *Rolling Stone Monthly*, a little glossy fan club magazine published in Britain. We would endlessly discuss every minute detail about the Rolling Stones.

When the Stones arrived in Sydney for their 1965 tour they hit town big time! The establishment was totally outraged that this group of antichrists had even been allowed entry into Australia. The Beatles had caused enough of a stir, but they were such wimps when compared to the Stones.

David used his pay cheque to procure a room in the Chevron Hotel in Potts Point, where the Stones were staying, and his Movietone News journalist's pass helped us move around the hotel without suspicion. Security was very tight, because fans would go to any lengths to get near the band. Girls were found crawling up air-conditioning chutes and hiding in laundry baskets.

Anyway, despite the security, no one ever questioned us. We took ourselves up to the next floor, and immediately found Stones' guitarist Brian Jones, sitting playing a zither on his bed, the door wide open. I'll never forget how sad he looked. Brian just sat there idly strumming his zither with the most tragic, faraway look in his eyes, seemingly oblivious to Ross and me. (Looking back on this, I do concede that it was possible the poor guy just had a shocking hangover.) Oddly, he turned out to be perhaps one of the nicest and most generous human beings, spiritually speaking, I've ever met. He actually seemed relieved, maybe even elated, by our presence. I do recall him trying to describe to us the disorientating and unnatural experience of being part of a famous rock group touring the world. Brian was not handling it at all! Quite frankly, he was a mess, and I felt great sadness for him. Experiences like this at a formative stage of your life really stay with you.

Let me briefly describe the rest of my day with the Rolling Stones. I made off down the hall to find guitarist Keith Richards, and find him I did, with no difficulty. Keith was a much more exuberant character than Brian, full of life, the happiest person in their entourage. I'm sure this is why Keith is still alive today, despite all the drugs. I chatted to Keith for hours about my aspirations to become either a graphic designer or a rock musician in London. I had brought along a pencil sketch I had drawn of the Stones; Keith said he thought it was great. (I'm not so sure about that, but as I said, Keef was a real gentleman!)

Later that afternoon, I bumped into drummer Charlie Watts and Bill Wyman, their bassist, also absolute gentlemen. I was stunned at how completely unaffected these guys were. (I have since learnt that successful people don't need to prove anything.) Charlie Watts was such a regular kinda guy, I can't even remember what we talked about. But I do recall that he took a real shine to Ross and me, and invited us to hitch a ride to that night's gig at the Sydney Showground in his limo. Fantastic.

The plan was this: we were to go up to Charlie's room at eight o'clock and then he'd accompany us down to the basement where a fleet of limos would be waiting to ferry the Stones to the gig. Ross and I were just on our way back downstairs when Mick Jagger returned from a shopping trip in the city.

'WHO ARE THESE LITTLE FUCKERS?' he screamed upon sighting us.

'Excuse me, Mick, could I get an autograph?' inquired Ross, a tad naively.

'NO! FUCK OFF!' Jagger yelled back. 'Get these little fuckers out of here and go find me harps!' screamed Jagger, referring to his harmonicas.

Keith and Brian both sprang to our defence, but it made no difference: there was absolutely no doubt who was the bossy boots of this seemingly autonomous band. We left and decided to stay invisible for a while.

We returned at around 8 p.m., regardless of Mick, and Charlie was genuinely glad to see us. We took the lift with

Charlie and Bill, but alas, we stopped a couple of floors down, the doors opened and in stepped Mick Jagger.

Ross, for some reason, decided the time was right to ask Mick why he recorded two versions of the song 'Everybody Needs Somebody to Love'. I felt acutely embarrassed. Jagger mercilessly ridiculed us, and we were abruptly turfed out of the lift on the ground floor, and had to go to the gig in a taxi. Looking back, I'd have to say that Mick Jagger is the most obnoxious rock star I have ever met, whereas the other four Stones must have been among the nicest people I have ever met.

Regardless, at the Showground that night I had one or two experiences I shall never forget. American crooner Roy Orbison was the support act and performed impeccably, as one would expect. I found myself seated next to a gorgeous teenage girl, who squealed rather impishly at the Big O, but once the Stones broke into song this nubile nymphet lost control. When Jagger bounded onto the stage a little after the rest of the band, this vision of loveliness grabbed me around the neck and dragged me down onto the floor of the venue.

Meanwhile, back at the ranch, there was a tiny but very loud group of Australian rock bands making a nuisance of themselves, despite the establishment's disdain and attempts to gag these *enfants terribles*. They had such cool names: The Easybeats, The Wild Cherries, The Loved Ones. I had led such an isolationist life, shut away in an Anglican boarding school, cut off and 'protected' from such decadence, apparently for my own good.

My first memory of seeing the legendary Easybeats was at an archetypical teenage nightclub in the centre of Sydney—complete with a huge spinning mirrorball. To me, it was total adolescent exhilaration. This was the life for me! I immediately fell under the spell of the 'cool'; we all wore long hair and dressed ourselves in 'Britpop' Carnaby Street clothes (or second-rate imitations). It was also mandatory to adopt a fake London accent. Fortunately, because of my schooling, I was able to actually speak with a London accent. This was way cool!

Back then, there were two main opposing gangs, the 'sharpies' and the 'long-hairs'. The feuding between these two factions was ugly and frequent and bloody. I remember going to see Billy Thorpe and the Aztecs at Surf City, a cavernous beer barn at the top of Kings Cross, where you'll now find the Crest Hotel. I had gone into the gig with my schoolmate Ross. A sharpie girl deposited herself firmly in my lap and began running her hands through my hair and making obscene suggestions. Suddenly, she changed into a vixen, whacking me over the head with her bag and screaming to her sharpie boyfriend that I had tried to molest her. It was an ambush, a set-up!

In the ensuing pandemonium, Ross was held down by five or six sharpies and kicked repeatedly in the ribs, the back, the kidneys and the teeth—which cost his parents a small fortune to have repaired. I was being held by a few sharpies myself; I distinctly remember screaming that there were almost twenty of them against two of us. I was terrified. Very real damage was being done to Ross and myself. The bouncers were MIA. I broke free, picked up a heavy metal chair and went into a frenzy, flailing the chair at literally anything or anyone that moved.

When I was a teenager, I had the shit kicked out of me more times than I care to remember and I can tell you that the feeling of some bastard's steel-capped boot connecting with your bloodied lips and crashing into your teeth, or some other cretin threatening to end your life with a bowie knife, ain't no fun. There is no honour—no machismo—just a lot of unbelievable pain. In a fleeting moment of madness you can inherit a lifetime of medical problems. Then again, I presume that if more people had their faces smashed in at an early age, there may be less violence in the world now.

I never did get to see Billy Thorpe and the Aztecs that night; the last thing I remember was Ross and me being chased out of Surf City by half a dozen bouncers.

I have so many recollections of Sydney nightlife in the late sixties; most of it is pretty nasty. The sharpies ruled, and the establishment backed them to the hilt. There were numerous incidents in Sydney (and Melbourne, for that matter), where long-hairs were regularly, brutally bashed and the police and judiciary would simply turn a blind eye. In the courts of 'justice' the pillars of the community convoluted the truth or just blatantly condemned long-hairs as aliens who had no right to co-exist with the rest of the 'respectable' community. One judge ruled that a sharpie who had brutally murdered a long-haired boy outside a city nightclub was far too respectable looking to have been guilty. The judge consequently let the murderer go free, despite damning evidence. (As I recall, the media discovered that the victim was actually the son of a Methodist minister; he attended church every Sunday and never touched alcohol or any other drug.)

I learnt to play 'Satisfaction' by the Rolling Stones before even buying my first guitar. My close friends from school had long dreamed of forming a band, becoming lifelong compadres and 'serious' musicians. We had been weaned on a rather elitist diet of black music: the blues of Muddy Waters, Howlin' Wolf and Willie Dixon, then later, the pure soul of Curtis Mayfield, The Four Tops, Marvin Gaye and Smokey Robinson. I was more obsessed with music than my friends, however, so I soon found myself with an imaginary band—if you know what I mean.

My group of friends, including my schoolmate Ross, had a fantastic notion of the 'beatnik' lifestyle, which we associated with artists of all genres. So, almost immediately upon escaping school, we moved en masse into a rat-infested dump of a flat right at the hub of Kings Cross, just near the El Alamein fountain. We soaked up the reckless decadence of the Cross like sponges. We thought it uncool to bathe, or wash our hair or clothing, so we didn't! We drank cheap spirits every night, played the first album by Americans The Byrds very loudly and partied hard and fast. We loved the numerous bohemian haunts in and around the Cross, places like the Trocadero jazz club, where I used to marvel over local jazz greats John Sangster and Judy Bailey. There was a fantastic coffee house not too far down William Street, a spawning ground for academics and intellectuals. I was in the thick of it.

Probably the most significant milestone of the time was my bumpy introduction to Bob Dylan. As I have already said, I had developed fairly sophisticated musical tastes by the time I was fifteen or sixteen. Ross's older brother returned from a couple of years of postgraduate study in Europe, bearing a few Dylan albums. I think I had heard Dylan's music but had been singularly unimpressed. Ross and I were a little drunk when Allan came down to his parents' recreation room bearing the LP *Bringing It All Back Home*. Ross and I were reeling in horror at Dylan's voice—after Smokey Robinson and Marvin Gaye, this Dylan guy really was too much. Allan forced us to sit through the song 'It's All Over Now, Baby Blue', and suddenly something clicked for me; it was like I was rebirthing. I still vividly remember the tidal wave of emotion that snuck up and swept me right away. I became an obsessive Dylan addict for many, many years after that. A couple of years later, when I was in London, the only panacea for sleep was to put both sides of Dylan's *Blonde on Blonde* LP on a self-changing record player and drift into a deep sleep to the epic 'Sad-Eyed Lady of the Lowlands'.

As pleasant as this brief period was, I knew I had to get out and live in the real world. Get a job. My aim was to scrape together a boat fare to England. In 1968 I worked for a brilliant graphic designer in North Sydney named Allen. I jumped straight into the work with great gusto and moved into a tiny bedsit in Neutral Bay, down near the ferry wharf. A female graphic artist, Gerri, was employed in the studio and I was her assistant. I loved this job, and my one-room hovel overlooking the harbour. I dined on an odd assortment of canned food that I would cook up in a ghastly aluminium saucepan. But it felt good being so independent for the first time in my life.

There was a crazy man in the neighbourhood who always wore the same expensive brown hat, and had strange steely blue eyes that seemed to always be looking skywards. He talked very erratically to himself as he rode the Neutral Bay ferry.

Gerri and I made friends quickly and easily. We were both aware that the very talented man who was employing us was a hopeless alcoholic; he was drinking himself into an early grave. The way he ran his business was equally tragic; we'd often wait weeks to be paid. Just as we were ready to quit, he would reappear after another mysterious absence. I stayed there maybe six, seven months. I was on a mission and time was marching on. I had to find more stable employment.

I then worked as a graphic artist in a large photography firm in the city, and lied my way into a job as a trainee management exec for Myer department store. Both of these jobs were fairly mundane, but at Myer I did befriend a fellow trainee management executive, Grant, who I met up with again when I got to London. I was fired from Myer and was still desperately trying to scrape together the boat fare to England.

Somewhere at this time I had also stumbled into a vague and platonic relationship with a girl called Lois, who'd been the girlfriend of Ross, my best friend from school. For a very brief period, when Ross and I were trying to emulate Bob Dylan and Allen Ginsberg by living in our bug-infested Kings Cross garret, Lois became part of our fantasy world. Being both attractive and an intellectual, she became our golden prize.

We would hang out with Lois's friends in the coffee houses around Kings Cross, and I'd fantasise about being a bohemian in one of Picasso's paintings. I was just longing to get to Paris and London.

However, things took a couple of weird twists and turns. Lois became pregnant to Ross—and much to my chagrin, he disappeared. No one, his family included, had a clue where he'd gone. One day I received a postcard from him: he was in Graz, Austria, working as a street sweeper. His father was furious, and Lois was totally shattered; she consequently had an abortion and clung to me for support. It was very sad.

I grabbed a quick job, clerking for a couple of months in the taxation office. It was one of the more bizarre experiences of my short life. The tax office was located in the city, and I had never before experienced such a bunch of rogues and layabouts. I don't remember any work ever actually being done. I only remember the drugs—amphetamines, and pharmaceuticals such as cough medicine, which contained opiates. I remember a bunch of fellow workers rifling through Mick Jagger's private tax files. I can still see my fellow workers totally catatonic on a cocktail of drugs.

I got out of there as soon as I possibly could. I lost hundreds of dollars in a phone booth and thought it was the end of my life until, much to my elation, the money was returned. Clearly my luck was in so I headed down to the office of the steamship company posthaste.

2

'But I won't come back,
Even if I live to be a thousand years'

i Wanna Be a Survivor

I booked myself a one-way ticket on the *Achille Lauro*, a fine old Italian ship. Lois decided to come with me, in pursuit of Ross. It's hard to describe to the uninitiated how incredibly romantic travelling by ship was. In 1967, you could sail to Europe in old-style luxury for a few hundred dollars.

I don't think Lois and I even had anybody to see us off, but it felt so good sailing out through the Heads at dusk, to destinations unknown. We befriended a funny hippie guy called Robert, who still lives somewhere down on the NSW South Coast.

Immediately upon disembarking in Cape Town, it hit us that any preconceived image we had had about South Africa and its apartheid regime was way too moderate. I was impressed that Bobby went out of his way, all day long, to shove it up those really stupid white Afrikaners. If the top deck of the bus was 'coloureds only', then we would sit up there; if the signs said 'coloureds only' in the department store, then we would go there and hurl abuse at the little white piggies with their little piggie wives. A disgusting place.

The rest of the voyage now seems more like a romantic 1950s Technicolor movie than a real part of my life. Mealtimes on board were always a special treat; the Italian waiters dressed impeccably, in white gloves and royal blue uniforms. The food was always fabulous and served with so much finesse. We stopped at Dakar on the westernmost tip of Africa; it was like being on the expedition to find Doctor Livingstone (I presume). We also went to the Canary Islands, which became one of my all-time favourite destinations. The capital Tenerife is almost like a Spanish colony from last century, frozen in time. The locals even took siestas. If I never had to work again, I would buy a little villa there with shuttered windows and sit on a white cane chair at my front door and chat to all the locals strolling down the cobbled streets, heading for the fish market. The life!

The *Achille Lauro* arrived at Southampton on a still autumn night. I was almost out of my skin with excitement. Fortunately for me, Her Majesty's Immigration Officer was good humoured and amiable.

'How long do you plan to stay?' he asked.

'I'm not sure,' I replied.

'How much money do you have for your stay?'

'Fifty quid.'

He chuckled politely.

'You're a really funny chap,' he said, and stamped my passport for twelve months.

Lois and I scurried onto the first train we could find, heading for London. Ross, who knew we were on our way, was now living in Fulham in a rather large flat with a few very yuppie Londoners (yuppies before their time, that is). The reception was a little strange. I had by this time slept with Lois, but Ross, I think, believed that he and Lois would automatically renew *their* relationship.

Consequently, it was all too complicated and Lois and I went on a search for alternative accommodation, ASAP. Still, I felt elated at simply being in London. Then there was the light—if you know London, the soft and beautiful light strikes you immediately, the way it bathes the courtyards in a sort of black and white halftone wash.

Anyway, we found a place in a house on Anson Road, Kilburn. Our landlords were Joe Panzer and his wife. It was just one big room; a piece of latticework separated the bed from the stove. I'm sure many of you who have lived in London know the exact set-up—the shared bathroom and toilet down the hall, and if you can't feed the gas meter, well, I guess you freeze to death!

Lois at this time was a fairly strict vegetarian; because we were relatively poor we stuck with the lifestyle. I look back with great nostalgia on those times in Kilburn. Joe Panzer and his wife were a lovely old Golders Green couple, almost surrogate parents to Lois and me. If I couldn't pay the rent because I'd spent too much money in the music shop, it was never a problem. If we asked to have something fixed, that was never a problem either.

We had so many blissful times, hitchhiking up to Oxford, Cambridge or Stratford-upon-Avon. I don't know what was in the water, but Lois and I made wonderful friends everywhere we went. Lois was working at the British Museum and was fast acquiring an Oxford accent; this, combined with her good looks, endeared her to everybody.

Yet our social circle was becoming strange and strained. In those days, rock music was the music of the common man. I was half acceptable, because at least I was intelligent enough to emulate Dylan's style of songwriting. But I was also into Jimi Hendrix and The Kinks and The Who. I couldn't stand the academic snobs we met, who really didn't have a decent knowledge of contemporary music.

Lois started to date academic professorial-type boyfriends because we were supposed to be a liberated hippie couple, into giving each other space and freedom. Besides, we had had a strange beginning with Ross.

This is probably where I became a more level-headed and sceptical hippie. I'd get jealous because that is my nature, and it very slowly started eating away at our relationship. I did, however, discover the cathartic powers of songwriting, and learned how I could exorcise my demons with words and music.

I went out looking for work. The most absurd job I applied for was a trainee executive gig at one of Europe's most prestigious merchant banks. For the second time in my short life, I used my fancy boarding school background to great advantage—without having to actually validate my education. I lied about matriculating, wore an immaculate suit, and I got the job. I was actually fired after a short time, but they paid me out handsomely, giving me enough funds to live for some time. I was determined to become a top graphic designer or illustrator; that was my real goal.

I got a job as a designer of a monthly radio communications magazine for the Radio Society of Great Britain. This was much like a real Fawlty Towers. It really was that loopy. There was Chris, the John Cleese-like boss; Dave, the skinhead Cockney mail boy; Elly, the cross-eyed Spanish accountant. Seriously. And there were a couple of other characters, including an old lady who had survived London during the Blitz and Anna, a German woman who'd been in the Hitler Youth when she was fourteen. (Anna explained to me that to be a Hitler Youth girl was no different to being a Girl Guide; in fact, in Germany in 1936, the Hitler Youth *was* the Girl Guides.)

I worked there for two very happy years. I designed the magazine each month, laid it out and cut out and pasted up strips of type and photos. It was such a cushy job that I was also able to attend St Martin-in-the-Fields Art School two nights a week, go and see several amazing gigs each weekend, and place ads in the *Melody Maker* looking for musicians to form bands.

All my memories of this time are warm and fuzzy. I loved London. I didn't even mind dragging myself out of bed each morning and dashing across the icy cold floor to pump coins into the gas meter. Then I rode the bus to Central London each morning; the Radio Society was located close to Tottenham Court Road. The downside was that after a while, I began to feel like a wage slave.

Elly, the Spanish accountant, was considerably older than me, having grown up under Franco, the terrible Spanish dictator. Not only was she ultra conservative in her attitude but she was obsessed with what I thought of as stupid Catholic morals. As you might have noticed by now, I had gone to great lengths to be the antithesis (or antichrist if you prefer) to Elly. I wasn't just a proud hippie, I was belligerent, too. However, as human experiments go, over a longish period, Elly and I became the best of friends. She cried when we finally parted ways some years later. We are conditioned to believe that all the nationalities are different and opposing tribes. We are indoctrinated to believe that there needs to be this imaginary delineation, thereby justifying wars and killing.

I remember her disdain for my long hair from the first day we met. I was thinking: 'Oh yeah, you Spanish fascist, you wanna take me on!' Yet when we scratched away at the surface, we found we were able to communicate emotionally; she became like a big sister figure to me. Ultimately, we grew into soul mates.

Dave the mail boy, however, was a different story. Most Monday mornings, thuggish, antisocial 'bovver boy' Dave wouldn't make it into work. If you are wondering why he wasn't fired, well, I did say this place was as eccentric as Fawlty Towers, and Chris the boss was super eccentric. He was a real softie; I don't think he had the heart to fire Dave.

Chris used to walk around the office muttering 'subs... subs'—I had no idea what it meant. Elly had to finally tell me that it had something to do with sub-totals. Anyway, I had to ask Dave what he did every weekend, although he was guarded about his private life. But Elly and I had broken down barriers, and now Dave and I were about to embark on our own journey.

Dave, you see, came from the East End, a rough part of London—he hated everyone and everything. He hated hippies, he hated the world. Why? Because everything was fucking hopeless, hopeless, hopeless; no future, no hope. I once saw Keith Moon from The Who interviewed, and he said that when you were growing up in the rougher parts of London in the sixties, you had two choices: become a pop star or spend your life in jail.

As it had been with Elly, Dave and I were quite hostile to each other at first; we were from two warring tribes. After a few weeks of his Monday disappearing act, I forced an answer out of him. I was pissed off that this little twerp thought he was so special as to have problems that I would not be able to understand.

His answer was simple. Every weekend, Dave and his mates followed one of the London soccer clubs—I think it was Fulham—and they would drink themselves into oblivion. Then, irrespective of what was going on in the match, he and his gang of bovver boys would start punching anything that moved. Blood and gore would be flying every which way, then the Bobbies would step in to break it up. This was Dave's favourite bit. He just wanted to kill coppers. (If ever police deserved my profound sympathy, it was right then.) Consequently, Dave spent most weekends in the police lock-up.

I recoiled in disgust and horror at this stupid boy, but my curiosity and compassion got the better of me. I persisted and Dave began to try to explain himself to me. Gradually the crap started to melt away and he burst into a torrent of tears. Dave had never cried before. He'd never talked to anyone in this way. I won myself a new friend.

During my two years at the Radio Society, I became more and more entranced by music and by musicians. My passion for artwork was being eclipsed by an overwhelming desire to be a musician. I was deep into my Dylan period by now. It's important to note that Bob Dylan gave birth to The Byrds, who together and singularly were the strongest formative influence in the *craft* of my music.

But this was London 1967! What a time. Virtually every gig I saw was simply incredible. I think perhaps Pink Floyd with Syd Barrett one Saturday night at the UFO Club, the biggest 'underground' club in England, might have been the pick. Pink Floyd's music is not necessarily my favourite, but I loved the all-consuming atmosphere that the audience created at Floyd gigs. Their gigs were more akin to an LSD trip than a mere concert. I didn't take acid, but didn't need to. I just had to see the Floyd.

I was so fortunate; just as I was becoming a musician in the true sense, there I was, in the midst of an era we'll never see again. I believe that this was rock music's *L'Age d'Or*, its Golden Age.

Try this for size: I saw Cream; Jimi Hendrix; Traffic; Emerson, Lake & Palmer; Fleetwood Mac (with guitarist Peter Green); Bob Marley; Ten Years After; Howlin' Wolf; Muddy Waters; The Faces—Rod Stewart with Jeff Beck, Ronnie Wood and Ronnie Lane; Deep Purple; Joe Cocker; John Mayall; Joe Walsh's first band, The James Gang; plus The Nice and many, many, more. Such an amazing time.

One of the more memorable gigs was seeing the Rolling Stones in Hyde Park, London, on 5 July 1969, mourning Brian Jones's death. Musically, this was a fairly awful-sounding gig, yet the event itself was absolute magic. I remember the whole day quite vividly. Despite my aversion to drugs, I thought the druggies (virtually everyone except the ambulance officers) were so cool. Even though I didn't imbibe, I still remember the afternoon as having this slow motion, LSD kind of vibe. Even the afternoon light in Hyde Park seemed surreal, like you were looking through a star filter.

At Sydney in 1965 there was so much screaming it drowned out the sound of the Rolling Stones. In Hyde Park, they were playing through a very loud PA system, yet they sounded awful. As their biggest fan, I figured that they had been through a hell of a lot that week—they were more of a family than just a band—so this must have been totally devastating for them. They were excused. The Shelley poem that Jagger read, dedicated to Jones, and the hundreds of butterflies they released into the park was an overwhelming emotional experience. There I was, surrounded by many thousands of people with tears welling up in their eyes, right in the centre of London. It was quite a contrast to the grumpy, uptight, pinstripe and bowler-hatted fools I saw on the Tube every morning. A real moment.

Describing the scene at the UFO Club is more difficult. If you have seen 1960s art movies like *Blow-Up*, and remember the scene where Jeff Beck is smashing his guitar, then that makes it much easier for me—that is a reasonable depiction of clubs like the UFO. Like all nightclubs it was smoky and dark and sweaty, with this kind of psychedelic vibe in the air. Everyone walked around as if they were treading on clouds, a sort of trance-like walk. Everyone's body language was warm and welcoming. I was probably under some sort of influence myself. It always seemed like the bright yellow sun was shining, even at midnight. (Honest officer, I've never taken LSD in my whole life!)

I think that one of the greatest performers I saw was blues legend Howlin' Wolf, whom I saw play a few times. It's weird how the intelligentsia treated these old guys with such pomposity. I loved watching Howlin' Wolf because he was an absolute riot! My favourite gig was at London University, where he was terrorising the pretty young girls down the front of the stage. They'd come along expecting this profoundly serious blues man, but instead were set upon by a sixty-five-year-old maniac. He'd roll around the stage with his legs up in the air (not easy, given that the guy weighed about 135 kilos) and terrorise his female fans by waving a phallic-looking Shure 57 microphone as he sang about his 'wang dang doodle'. He always used the same bunch of white London players; they really whipped up a storm. Tragically, Chester Burnett passed on shortly after the last time I saw him at London Uni. He left quite an impression, though.

There are so many other gigs to rave about. Fleetwood Mac's Peter Green on stage with his white robes and long curly black hair, adopting a Jesus stance after every song, like something straight off a Catholic postcard. Jeff Beck at a jam-packed Manor House, the best blues/R'n'B pub in England, hell-bent on some destruction. Oh, I must tell you about this! His *guitar lead was crackling,* and for whatever reason—drugs, bad temper, who knows—Beck rammed his guitar through his speaker cones one at a time. There were maybe twenty-four cones in all, and yes, he managed to ram his guitar through every single one. Then he smashed his guitar into bits.

Yet the master of all this mayhem had to be Pete Townshend. I saw The Who at Hammersmith Odeon, where I had managed to score front row seats. The James Gang, Joe Walsh's band before the Eagles, was supporting. These guys really were awesome, as in fucking gargantuan. They produced the most enormous wall of sound I had ever heard. The Who then came on like a cyclone. They were fit to kill. During Townshend's trademark windmilling attacks on his guitar, I was splattered with his blood. He had a full glass of whisky on top of his amplifier; between songs he'd plunge his bloody hand into the Scotch and then rape the guitar again. If you've ever seen a recording of a tornado, and remember the rumbling sort of sound, a prelude to all the fury that follows, then that's as good a description as I can give you of The Who. I'll remember this gig for the rest of my life. Their legendary *Live at Leeds* album was from the same tour.

Before turning into some encyclopaedia of British rock— just what the world needs—I have to mention seeing Blind Faith live in Hyde Park, the most soulful performance I'd seen from any act for many years. I saw Cream, Eric Clapton's band before Blind Faith, in the gymnasium at London University, but it was a bummer, a cacophony of white noise. I also saw Bob Marley live at the Lyceum. You can actually see Lois in video footage of that show—she was right down the front of the stage in front of Marley. I used to go to the Rainbow, the Manor House, the Marquee Club—I'm fairly sure there wasn't any London venue I didn't visit numerous times.

Not surprisingly, I was starting to play some music myself. A chap named Nigel was my first guitar player; the guy was a genius who could emulate B.B. King so well sometimes you would swear he was the King. We played together for a year or so, I guess, until Nige scored a better, bigger gig. Our time together was pretty uneventful, though; I was still very intimidated.

One day after work, I was admiring a beautiful black Telecaster guitar in a music shop on Shaftesbury Avenue. It was incredibly cheap and the egotistical salesman (you know, salesman to the stars) wouldn't tell me why this wonderful guitar was being flogged off so cheaply. Nigel was one of those boffins who knows everything there is to know about guitars, so I gave him a call and asked him to come down and help me out.

Nigel wouldn't take any crap from the obnoxious salesman; he demanded to take the guitar outside into the twilight, despite the salesman's protestations. Nigel held it up to the light, and let out a 'gotcha!' He came bounding back into the shop, and nailed the salesman.

'Whose guitar was this, man?' he asked. 'Townshend? Beck? Blackmore? Ah ha, yes! It is Ritchie Blackmore's, isn't it? See this hairline fracture all the way down the guitar, man—Blackmore smashed this on stage, didn't he?'

Nigel turned to me. 'This guitar isn't worth shit now. Come on, let's get out of here.'

Thanks, Nige.

I placed ads in *Melody Maker* for players to help form my first band. Drummer Steve Dixon was my first amigo. Steve, like Dave the mail boy, was a tough Londoner. Although he initially showed a lot of hostility towards all humanity, as soon as I told him what a great drummer he was, it dissipated. We then found Mick, a Cockney guitarist, and Barry, his best mate and our new bass player.

These were the two most colourful and unreal characters in all of London. I have to draw a parallel with the characters in the movie *Spinal Tap*; Mick and Barry must have been the inspiration. Whenever I think of them I also think of the immortal poetry of Derek and Clive, the comic alter egos of Peter Cook and Dudley Moore: 'Larf—I nearly shat!' Mick and Barry had hair down to their bums and very loud, very obscene Cockney accents. Every sentence was punctuated with 'fuckin' cunt'. They hated pot-smoking hippies but loved sculling twenty pints o' bitter down the pub. I might have been a hippie but they loved me because I was an Aussie—they thought Aussies were so cool 'cause they drank so much piss.

We started rehearsing constantly. I was writing as hard and as fast as I could, although the beauty of being a support band—which is what we were—is that we only needed about half an hour's worth of material. As I recall, we only played my tunes, yet the only song of mine I can clearly remember was called 'Mister Fysh', the first song I wrote. I think the inspiration was something scandalous that happened to a gay blade who owned a shirt shop in Savile Row called (you guessed it) Mister Fysh. I can't even remember how the song goes, which proves how memorable it must have been. I do know that we recorded the song; someone, somewhere must have an acetate.

3

'Burn, burn down your bridges,
While you still got the time,
Burn, burn down your bridges,
Look ahead, not behind'

Burn Down Your Bridges

Because I was the bandleader, I went out and bought an old Ford Transit van, the 'in' vehicle for all London rock bands. I don't drive nowadays and it's remarkable that I managed to drive this thing accident-free all over London and southeast England. We'd play for 20 or 30 quid per gig, and only ever played unis and colleges.

I didn't want to be seen as some long-haired fairy, so I used to force that revolting English beer down my gullet, just to be one of the boys. But London was the hub of the universe and there were some magic nights down the pub, packed to the rafters with we smelly, sweaty drunks, some 200 of us, arm in arm, belting out 'All Right Now' by Free or, better still, 'Lola' by The Kinks. To hear 'Waterloo Sunset' by the Kinks while walking across Waterloo Bridge at sunset remains one of the great memories of my life.

That laughter is perhaps the thing I remember most about London in the sixties. And I mean laughing till you're pissing your pants, tears rolling down your cheeks, holding your tummy because it hurts so much. That's how it was, night after night down the pub—even better, back then we never got hangovers. Maybe all the laughter was simply because I was still so young; I'd yet to be shackled with the responsibilities of adult life. Maybe.

Every Tuesday night was *Monty Python* night and we would religiously pick up the beer from the off licence and settle in. Watching *Monty Python* with my little band of Cockney merry men probably heightened the experience two-fold. Every part of my body would ache like hell afterwards.

Through Steve Dixon, I was fortunate enough to spend a lot of time at Dick James Music during Elton John's early days there, and later at Apple, the Beatles' record label. Dick James was the Beatles' music publisher. For a kid with such a disadvantaged background, Steve was a very together young man, and he landed himself a position as James's general dogsbody. This was thrilling for both of us; it was the happening place to be that year.

Every night after work I'd walk up to meet Steve at the studio; I loved the whole atmosphere of the place. Steve was always trying to talk me up because he really believed in me. His loyalty was rock solid and permanent; he'd do anything for me.

Later on, Steve moved to Apple as an assistant engineer. How cool was that? I could walk in and out of Apple Records any time I wanted, and because of Steve, was always made to feel comfortable in this hallowed palace of the Beatles.

The Beatles themselves would regularly come and go, and although I can't claim to have actually hung out with them, I would sometimes manage a very sheepish 'hi'. It was just an absolute buzz to actually be hanging around Apple; I knew I was living out a dream. (Sadly, no, I wasn't there when they played on the roof.) Steve's career was going from strength to strength, and I can't recollect exactly what happened, but with no animosity, he and I decided to call it a day. We stayed friends, but were no longer bandmates.

Mick and Barry and I were auditioning new drummers, and a thin weedy little guy with John Lennon glasses turned up. It was Micky Waller, who was Rod Stewart's drummer and the top session player in London. That afternoon, I didn't know who he was until he started playing in that slightly open, hi-hat style of his. I was blown away. Micky was a lovely guy, but declined to join our band; he did, however, say that he'd always be there for us if we were ever stuck.

We ended up with a guy called Steve Rose, who'd just left some big time pop band and was a real pop star himself. But the work dried up for a while, as it does, and the band started to fall apart. I vaguely remember playing at private parties and college gigs. I still have a photo of that line-up; it's only a clipping from a proof sheet, but I must have spent quite a bit of money on the photo session. We must have been trying to get *somewhere*.

After a couple of years, in 1969, I decided to leave the Radio Society, and I landed a graphic designer job at Swifts, the largest printers in the UK. I earned 38 quid a week, unheard of for a young artist—family men weren't earning this much, so I was doing OK. The two key characters in this scenario were Pam, a pretty blonde East Ender, also a graphic designer, and Emerson, a Jamaican compositor who could type faster than anyone I have ever known; he was the best comp in London, hands down.

I was now a freewheeling bachelor, looking for accommodation. Emerson, who had taken an immediate liking to me, asked me to move in with him. So I moved into Kensal Green, the original black suburb of London, way before Notting Hill Gate. This was the most interesting time I had during my stay in England. Among the many people living there was Robert, who I think had known Emerson in school, and Marva, a vivacious black girl with a big sunshiny smile, her teeth brilliantly white. She always had a smile to light up your day—she always made me feel good.

They lived life by Rasta. We had reggae music on non-stop. Emerson fancied himself as a bit of a musician and wanted to quit Swifts and form a reggae band with me. We never did, though; we were both making far too much money at the printers.

Every morning, I'd stumble sleepily downstairs to find Marva and the boys cooking breakfast in perfect time to the music. If they were frying toast or flap jacks, they would fling them in to the air at the end of the first bar and the food would land back in the pan perfectly in time with the second bar. I've never known such happy people. They lived by the creed, 'Don't worry—be happy', and this was 1969, way before Bobby McFerrin made it a hit single. And no, I don't think I have ever met a miserable Jamaican!

Every morning Emerson and I would scurry off down to the Kensal Rise Tube station, and cram ourselves on to the crowded train. Emerson could honestly not understand why all the people looked like they hated life so much. He'd want to chat to them in his beautiful Jamaican accent. We were such an odd couple—a lanky, chatty, well-educated Jamaican, and a short, white hippie in a suit, stirring things up every morning on the 8:05 to Tottenham Court Road.

'Are you happy with your life?' we'd ask the tightly wound locals, as they looked away. 'If you are,' we continued, 'let's see a nice big smile, because if you can learn to smile at people, they'll smile back at you. Before you know it, the whole world will be smiling, man!'

The silly prats in their pin stripes and bowler hats never did seem to get it.

Emerson and Pam started to have an affair. The bastard had told me that Marva was his ex-girlfriend; he was just helping her out with a place to live until she could find her own. It took me almost a year to discover that Marva was actually his wife, a quirk in male Jamaican attitudes that I can't explain. It was a whirlwind romance, and for many happy months the three of us would keep the art studio in stitches; the boss didn't mind because we were all excellent workers.

Emerson would have the radio on all day, waiting for a reggae song, so he could show off with his lightning fast typing. He really could type in reggae time. Pam and Emerson's relationship got a bit turbulent as the months went on, most of it triggered by Emerson's chauvinism. Many times at parties that were predominantly West Indian, Emerson would use Pam as his token white trophy. I began catching him playing up with girls in another part of the house while a very distraught Pam would be tearily looking for him. This was a tough time for me. Jamaican men are just like that, and who was I to be judgemental? Then again, when I took Emerson down the East End to meet Pam's father, it's difficult to say who had the most offensive attitude—Emerson the chauvinist, or Pam's ignorant father, who threatened to go back inside and get his cricket bat and smash our skulls in if we didn't go back to Mars or wherever he thought we came from!

I started a clandestine and highly passionate carnal relationship with Anne, the cute receptionist at Swifts. She was an archetypal East Ender, cheeky and provocative. She was also very primal; it was very much a case of the frisky bull chasing the heifer around the paddock—and that's the way she liked it. Friday was the big night out and it was these piss-ups down the local pub that led Anne and me into our clandestine night games.

She was a wild little tiger with a dirty mouth; I quickly became addicted to her. She was the only lover I have ever experienced who was into rough stuff—scratching, clawing, ripping off bras and pantyhose in the alleyway behind the pub, with lots of filth thrown in. She loved filth.

But she neglected to tell me she had a boyfriend, an unemployed thug from Shepherd's Bush. (Yes, my social circle in England was a bit of a dichotomy—my friends were either academics, or reprobates from the rough end of town.) This clandestine affair went on for a few weeks, and then I started getting weird phone calls, death threats, but only at work. I knew so few people—as compared to nowadays—and I really couldn't imagine who would want to kill me. I was very confused.

One night Anne got so drunk I had to take her home. As I was helping her up the stairs of Shepherd's Bush Tube station, her skinhead boyfriend was waiting with about half a dozen of his mates. I was about to have my head kicked in when a train pulled in, heading back to the city. I *just* managed to squeeze in through the automatic doors, leaving Anne's boofhead boyfriend and his mates screaming obscenities on the platform.

I decided to give Anne a big swerve after that, and she revealed herself as an unpleasant little vixen. One night at our house in Kensal Green, the boyfriend and two carloads of his mates turned up right outside.

'If you want bovver,' they bellowed at me, 'come downstairs!'

Now, I must say that the lads were getting in a bit deep. The only white people on the street were me and a little old Jewish couple who lived nearby. And my other West Indian mate, Robert, weighed in at over 110 kilos and was built like a brick shithouse.

Still, I did not want 'bovver'; Robert and Emerson almost had to push me outside to confront these boofheads. I went out alone. Anne's boyfriend and a couple of his mates jumped out of their car, pumped up and ready for a rumble. Just as they got close to me, Robert and another huge black mate of his came sidling up behind me.

'What business you got callin' on our Richie boy here?' Robert asked the white boys. 'Richie is our brother, mon, now don't you be callin' him bad names or saying bad things 'cause you make me and my friends very angry, mon!'

The bovver boys started slagging off Robert but then the two black giants jumped the little picket fence, and man, you couldn't see those scared white boys for the blue smoke that came screaming from their tyres. I never did hear from them again, and, not surprisingly, Anne quit her job.

Speaking of black friends, I also worked in Harrods department store as a storeman and packer one Christmas. I worked down in the bowels of Harrods, a bit like the little slaves in *Indiana Jones and the Temple of Doom*. My fellow inmates included Thomas, a Nigerian, who was already a graduate in industrial chemistry and was trying to work his way through another university degree. Thomas had one of the highest IQs of anyone I have met, and I've met some brilliant people. He was an outstanding academic. We had a dumb fuck white foreman, who delighted in treating us like enslaved rats. I was always at odds with this bastard.

The next few months are all a bit vague. I can't remember how I came to form a new band with two Californians and a Canadian, and I'm sure Steve Dixon returned to play drums with us at some stage. I do remember that it was such a great band I knew I was going to be a rock musician for life. These guys were into groups like Poco and The Flying Burrito Brothers, the whole country-rock scene. I can't remember their names, yet these guys changed my life. This became the musical genre that I'd finally settle into, despite an extreme musical detour a short time later in Berlin.

The next part of the story I will never forget.

The American band members, who were nineteen years old, just kids, had been smuggling pot from LA to London in aluminium film canisters, strictly for their own use. I was still firmly anti-drug, and quite frankly scared of anything that may make me lose control.

Lois and I, meanwhile, were still the best of friends, but decided it was better to remain as independent as we could. But we began an absurd situation in Earl's Court, where I moved after Kensal Green. I was living in the tiniest little bedsit, right next to Lois's rather more spacious bedsit—this is what we called living apart. One night there was a hell of a commotion from downstairs; I realised it was a police raid. They were busting Danuta, the young Polish landlady, for marijuana.

This was a fairly big block of flats; Lois and I lived on the fourth floor, very high up, while my bandmates were living downstairs. The cops then busted my new band for drug trafficking and started bashing on the door of my place, and also Lois's. They'd obviously had us under surveillance for quite some time, because they knew Lois and I were an item, that the Americans were in a band with me, and—get this—that Mick and Barry (remember them?) still lived in a rat-infested dump nearby. The cops knew I also had some sort of relationship with them.

There were about half a dozen uniformed Bobbies, sniffer dogs and two drug squad detectives. There was a bad cop and a good cop, naturally. They interrogated Lois and seemed convinced she was innocent, but the bad cop had it in for me. He continued to interrogate me despite my (valid) protestations. It seemed that because I had long hair I must be a drug addict, and that I was asking for trouble.

This bad cop was slapping me around and screaming in my face: 'Where's your stash? Where's your stash?'

I kept denying my guilt; I was most definitely innocent. When he discovered that I was Australian—a secret that Lois and I had kept well hidden—he demanded to see my passport.

He didn't believe I was Australian. This only made him angrier—there were long-haired quiffs like me 'down under an' all'? Shocking.

Then he threatened to plant pot in my room. He really didn't give a fuck—he was going to bust me and have me thrown out of the country, no matter what.

Next thing, bad cop slowly, methodically pushed me towards the window of Lois's room. I'm talking one hell of a drop to the street, probably 10 or 12 metres. Lois was screaming her head off; I was foolishly calling him a fucking arsehole—good one, Richard. Good cop was warning bad cop that he better haul me in, but by this time he had me hanging out the window by my ankles. I was scared shitless.

Fortunately, so was good cop, who screamed at bad cop to stop. This whole scene probably only lasted a couple of minutes but, as they say, to me it seemed like an eternity.

Good cop hauled bad cop outside for a serious reprimand. But bad cop was relentless and decided to drag me over to Mick and Barry's flat.

Keep in mind, despite the fact that these two looked like long-haired junkies, they were actually heavy metal dudes who hated hippie 'poofs' like me with a vengeance. My heart was full of dread.

Their door was so full of dry rot that when the Bobbies kicked it in the entire flat nearly collapsed. Bad cop charged into the dark like some big hero, shouting, 'POLICE!' He shook

Mick, still comatose from a big night. Thinking about it now, the next bit is like the funniest slapstick movie, but at the time it was terrifying. Bad cop shook Mick one too many times; Mick sprang out of bed and threatened to beat the ever-loving crap out of him. Barry soon joined in. Bad cop was trying to flash his badge, but Mick and Barry were pushing him up against a wall. Bad cop then shouted fatal words: he called them druggies. Oh dear.

Mick and Barry went berserk. When good cop finally restored some sort of order, he started giving bad cop a screaming reprimand, peppered with the sort of expletives you'd only hear from sailors. Good cop told us we were all free to go. He actually apologised for everything they'd put us through, and told us that bad cop must be a fuckin' idiot to be accusing Mick and Barry of being drug addicts.

This should have been the end. However, the next day a uniformed constable called in and told me that detective so and so had told him that my visa had long expired and I had until the end of the week to get out of Great Britain—or face arrest and deportation. The slimy bad cop made life almost impossible for me during the rest of my stay in Europe.

I decided to get out of the United Kingdom. I figured bad cop was going to be waiting for me around every bend. I'd had enough.

4

'And i saw jesus in the cornfield
Hanging from His cross'

Southern Germany

During my time in London, I became a passionate traveller. I hitchhiked all over Europe, from the south of France to the top of Denmark, and frequently found myself in West Berlin. Contrary to the popular caricature of the Germans, I met some fine people in Germany. I have fantastic recollections of hitching rides all over the Continent: with a German racing car driver who drove me from Hamburg to Munich in his Porsche at phenomenal speed; and with many wonderful truckies from all over Europe.

I don't think I have never known such warm hospitality as I found in Germany; perhaps the hippie revolution had made Samaritans of everyone. On one trip, I was on the road with Karl Marx von Schumann, a radical left-wing activist from Berlin. He struck me as very together in his thinking. Everything he told me about his political beliefs seemed very rational and very sound; it had a marked influence on me. It was therefore only natural that I appealed to him for help when I had the spot of bother with the British police.

SOUTHERN GERMANY

I bade farewell to all my English friends in 1970, headed for Berlin, keeping only my Gibson electric guitar (a Les Paul Junior) and a rucksack full of essentials. I headed off into the wild blue yonder, barely in my twenties, still young enough to be overwhelmingly elated and excited about this great new adventure. I had very little money, and no idea how I was going to survive.

Karl lived in a commune in Berlin. He was very hospitable at first, and because he lived his entire life by the communist ethos, I respected the rules of communal living. I worked my arse off doing the chores, and shared his disdain for hedonism and decadence (drugs and sex being the staple diet of my generation). We didn't go to nightclubs—our girlfriends were stern intellectual types who would come around for coffee and clandestine meetings plotting the overthrow of the decadent capitalist system.

Things began to get rather tense around the commune. I think Karl was conflicted: his political beliefs really urged him to support me as an unemployed foreigner, but his upper-middle-class background was like a devil on his shoulder, whispering: 'You don't need this shit—kick the foreign bastard out!'

We had a screaming argument one night, and, just like that, I was out on the street on the cusp of a freezing Berlin winter. I wandered the streets with no money and nowhere to go, sneaking in to bars for the most part, but being hustled back out on the street when they realised I had no money. I decided I would take a trip; people were so much kinder when I hitchhiked. Lois had a friend at Sydney University who had married a German doctor and settled down in the town of Paderborn. Her name was Denise. I had Denise's address so I thought I'd drop in on her.

Paderborn is probably the most deeply Catholic of all German communities. In fact Paderborners are a bit of a joke all over Germany; they are such caricatures of the perfect German Christian Democrat. Fortunately for me, Denise and her husband were great altruists who gave me shelter while I considered my future.

Quite frankly, I didn't have too many options. I was estranged from my family, and my best friends were scattered all over the world, so I didn't have much to look forward to in Australia. I had less hope of getting to North America, and really, Europe was my only home—now, without the option of Britain, Germany was my *only* home. I had no visas or permits, but at that time it was easy to just move into Germany and start a new life without them. My brief sojourn in Paderborn was a marvellous respite and gave me the chance to get sorted, make a plan.

I hit the road to get out and see more of Germany, especially the south. I wandered all over Hanover, Dusseldorf, Cologne and down into Bavaria. I had no money, yet as miraculous as this sounds, people would walk up to me in the street and give me 50 or 100 deutschmark. Quite often middle-aged *hausfrau* would thrust the money into my hand, with one instruction: 'Get a haircut.'

The people who would pick me up hitchhiking usually gave me money, and often they'd insist I stay in their spare bedroom for as long as I wanted. This may sound a bit fantastic, but in the late 1960s in Europe, especially Northern Europe, the hippie movement pervaded every strata of society. There was an unbelievable camaraderie that, sadly, we'll probably never see again.

Yet it was not all peace and love. One freezing night in a small Bavarian town I went to take shelter in an all-night bar, of which there are plenty in Germany. I met a friendly boy and girl who loaded me up on beer and bratwurst and *pommes frites*. I thought I was in for a wild night of *ménage à trois*. They invited me to stay at their place; I enthusiastically accepted. It was just starting to snow and the three of us drunkenly managed to cram onto the guy's moped and ended up at an abandoned warehouse on the outskirts of the town.

Now, drunk as I was, I started to worry. They ran laughing and screaming through the first two darkened floors of the warehouse and I followed them up to the third level. I could see a tiny slat of light way across the other side of the building. We made it into this strange big room, which they shared with another couple of young people, whose look strongly implied 'junkie'.

They rolled up a joint, claiming it was merely hash. I had by this time had a few tokes on joints, because Germans were drug crazy—smoking was unavoidable and inevitable. I was a little worried about these strange new friends but thought I'd better respect their hospitality. Within minutes I realised we were smoking opium, very common in Germany at the time.

I could feel hallucinations creeping in. Suddenly I noticed that my strange new friends were indulging in a weird ritual, heating up heroin in tarnished spoons, and I freaked. I went plummeting downstairs, across the pitch-black darkness of the warehouse. I didn't stop running until I was a safe enough distance away, and found refuge on a park bench. Finally, I slept.

The nightmares I had were like scenes from *Rosemary's Baby*. The next thing I knew a couple of highway patrolmen were escorting me to the outskirts of town.

'Don't come back,' they said, and walked away.

I wandered around Europe for some months. If you have read the final chapter of *Down and Out in Paris and London* by George Orwell—one of my main influences—you may recall his great description of agonising over his last shilling on a freezing night in Trafalgar Square. He decides to spend it in a doss house, so he can sleep; then he describes the feeling of total elation and liberty—he is finally free of every last penny.

Orwell described that feeling and experience perfectly. These were some of the happiest moments of my life. Not only was I really free, but my relaxed state seemed to bring out the best in everyone around me. I slept in farmers' barns in the south of France; the railway station at Copenhagen; Dam Square in Amsterdam. Everywhere I went, people were fantastically kind to me. I was invited to stay as long as I wanted in the apartment of a Danish dentist and his wife.

Strange as it must sound, my hosts never wanted me to leave. Not only did I survive but I managed to live out this dream existence without one pfennig—just heaps of human kindness.

I did make a serious attempt to put down some roots in Hamburg. It also made sense professionally because Hamburg had always been the music capital of continental Europe—that's where the Beatles really got started. I'd met a uni student while hitching; he had this beautiful house on Hamburg Harbour. Obviously from a well-to-do family and studying Chinese philosophy, he was also very 'hippie' so we got on well. I stayed at his place but didn't want to lose my independence. I took my leave and moved on.

I borrowed some money from friends in London and moved in temporarily with this crazy old man who'd been one of the foremost classical conductors in Germany in the 1930s. He was every inch the eccentric genius. Sheet music was stacked up to the ceiling in every room; I made my way around the house like a rabbit in a warren. He was a fascinating individual, but a victim, a survivor of terrible Nazi torture.

I didn't have much luck finding work in Hamburg and I kept missing Berlin. It felt like a second home to me and has ever since. The old orchestra conductor was very difficult to live with; he'd have fits and nightmares. I was just too young to deal with it. His idea of conversation was to scream at me in guttural German; I could barely understand him. I hit the road again.

I returned to Berlin with much trepidation. I'd had the most wonderful adventure out on the road, but after so many months of vagrancy I was now beginning to wonder if I would ever leave desolation row. Berlin was also a reasonably scary place to be a derelict; there were more psycho cases per capita than other areas of Germany, many of them screwed up World War II victims who drank themselves into oblivion. Then there were American GIs stationed in Germany, fresh out of Vietnam, smacked out on heroin.

Shuffling from bar to bar, I managed to sustain myself reasonably well for a number of days, befriending folk club patrons and playing them a song on my guitar. The hippies, with their sense of solidarity, were eager to help me out; they'd buy me food and beer and more often than not I would meet a girl and end up back at her place being treated to a bath or a shower—plus a free breakfast. It was just heaven, really!

I began making great friends all over Berlin. There were very few foreign hippies in the city, so I was a novelty. Germans held 'English' musicians in the highest esteem, so that helped, too.

I was very down on my luck, ran out of money and started to worry. I met a South American dude, who made fabulous leatherwork, and agreed to sell his work on Kurfürstendamm, Berlin's main street. I learnt the art of selling to tourists like a duck taking to water, even though I hated doing it. It's all confidence trickery; I'd set my own price. I'd sell a Berliner a belt for say, 50 deutschmark, but I could ask an American or Australian for 200 marks—and get it!

Consequently, I began making some money and feeling like a bona fide Berliner. I even adopted a slight German accent when I spoke—and I spoke mainly in German.

However, when my South American amigo left town I was broke again. I bit the bullet and went to the Australian Military Mission to ask for financial assistance. This was where I met Gisela, a former fashion model, now in her thirties and working at the Mission. Gisela used her contacts to arrange permanent residency and work papers for me.

Along with Gisela, I went to a left-wing students' commune in Klausenerplatz. It became my home for a long time. The key figure there was Volker, to this day one of my closest friends. Among the others at the commune was Uwe, a medical student from Linz and a natural born drug addict, and a couple, Georg and Sabine, also still very close friends. The commune may have been Marxist in principle, but these people were fun.

Volker, Uwe, Georgie and I would drink Stolichnaya until dawn, fight in the snow at 4 a.m. and then do wheelies in a little European car on the ice. We were the larrikins of Berlin. We played up at parties and got thrown out of bars and teased the prostitutes on Kurfürstendamm and got up to mischief every night. And there were girls. So many beautiful girls.

As the head of the commune, Volker told me very sternly that I must write songs and nothing but, or I'd be ostracised. The group supported me. We fed ourselves splendidly for a few marks a day. Volker and I would go to the market at Klausenerplatz and buy food wisely—subsequently we lived like kings, at least in the culinary sense.

Volker was an orthodox left-winger so our group was drug-free, but heavy vodka drinking and smoking cigarettes were permitted.

Volker and Georg were studying architecture at Berlin University; Uwe was studying medicine. Volker had access to just about everything at the uni and brought me home a terrific reel-to-reel recorder, a Revox. Thanks to Volker, I started on the songs for my first album, *Prussian Blue*, my first 'serious' attempts at songwriting, which would emerge in 1973, three years down the line. I only owned two cassettes at this time: Neil Young's *After the Goldrush* and David Crosby's solo album *If I Could Only Remember My Name*. I can definitely hear their influence on *Prussian Blue*.

Volker decided that he would manage me, and that together we'd build a socio-political propaganda machine. I thought that the Marxist Communist Manifesto was the only feasible proposition for the world's future, and embraced the philosophy wholeheartedly. Most of my early songwriting efforts were heavy with political messages.

During my early months in the commune, I feared I might be causing some consternation; I was totally dependent on the others for support. Gisela found me a job as greenkeeper for the British Embassy. Quite simply, all I had to do was mow the lawns every couple of weeks, and I could spend the rest of the time sitting in the sun writing lyrics. And the pay was excellent.

But when Gisela and I broke the good news to Volker, he threatened me with expulsion from the commune. His rationale was very simple.

'Songwriters write songs,' Volker insisted. 'That is that!'

Georgie, Uwe, Volker and I went out that night and got horribly drunk. They drilled into me one simple fact: they had enormous faith in my musical ability; they wanted to be my patrons. I agreed, even if their charitable attitude seemed odd at such an early stage in my development. But their patronage made me all the more conscientious. By late 1970, I had written songs like 'Poor Man's Saviour' and 'Southern Germany'. Georg and Volker, both Bavarians, were immensely proud of these songs, so it all went around and came back around.

Volker made a concerted effort to place me with the best musicians in Berlin. There was a left-wing band called Agitation Free that mainly hung out at Kommune Einz, the notorious breeding ground for radical political activists and, allegedly, members of the Baader-Meinhof gang. These weren't the cheeriest people, as you could imagine, so my early attempts to form a band were tainted by this pseudo intellectualism.

It's here I first made contact with Michael 'Fame' Gunther and Michael Hoenig, who later joined the legendary German art-rock band Tangerine Dream.

I can't exactly remember how we first stumbled across Burghard Rausch, our drummer, but being a real Anglophile, Burghard was the necessary bridge between me and 'Fame'. We were rostered on at the Hochschule für Musik (the Highschool for Music) and placed under the supervision of Professor Tomas Kessler, a protégé of the avant-garde composer Stockhausen.

The school had its own sixteen-track recording facility and featured many weird implements with which to make weird sounds. We were rostered on Tuesdays and Thursdays, and I'm forever grateful for this unique musical experience; I was able to immerse myself totally for almost two years and simply make music without all the extraneous bullshit that comes with being a professional musician. It was very pure.

At the Hochschule I really wanted to impress Professor Kessler—and stick it to Fame—and stated that I planned to learn Frank Zappa's 'King Kong', a bizarre piece of musical mayhem, about 20 minutes long, absolutely hell to play. I was being childish, but I succeeded in impressing Kessler and denigrating Fame (and Burghard, too, for that matter). I stubbornly managed to learn the entire piece and play it—but don't ask me to play it now! Not a chance.

Michael 'Fame' Gunther passed away in Berlin on 29 March 2014.

My two years in West Berlin were the happiest and most carefree of my life; the city was like an island of Western decadence behind the Iron Curtain. I can't recall meeting another Australian during my time there, and I didn't miss Australia until very late in my stay.

There was passionate activity everywhere; crazy Berliners creating music, books and magazines and films. The cutting-edge art movement was fantastic. There were eccentric technology boffins—1970s geeks—in garrets all over the city, inventing and designing amazing gizmos and concepts for different art forms. Volker was madly inventing weird devices to blow up Marilyn Monroe's lips to the size of a football field, along with other bizarre concepts.

Having just lived through the golden age of British rock music and mixed it with the English hippies, I was now living out the last days of classic Berlin, the cultural hub of the universe.

I was one lucky hippie.

5

'Then when i woke up in the
morning babe, you had flown'

Prussian Blue

Berlin coffee houses and bars were packed with intellectuals and beautiful women, and Volker, Uwe, Georgie and I savoured every moment. Bratwurst and *pommes frites* were wonderful, vodka was fabulous, women were celestial, artists were inspiring, arguments were fucking great fun; it was simply great to be alive. Maybe because we were so poor we were totally liberated—and so very much alive.

Georg and Sabine bought a beautiful house in Wannsee, and a brand new Citroën. Our hippie life was suddenly distorted by luxury items, material things—and we no longer lived on the commune. We used to go out and get roaring drunk and pull up next to old people at the traffic lights. Georg would then make the car's pneumatic suspension go up and down, up and down. The elderly Germans would be outraged at the sight of bedraggled hippies in a brand new Citroën.

One night, drunk again, we decided that we had to go to Munich in West Germany from Berlin in the East—it was a sort of pilgrimage. The East German border guards nearly arrested us;

we would have ended up in Siberia. They were frustrated that my papers were in order, that I was a bona fide Berliner. Regardless, they dragged me into a hut, held me down and were set to hack off all my hair. Luckily a senior officer saved me at the last minute.

We literally drank our way south to Munich, and how we weren't arrested in cafés and bars throughout East Germany still amazes me. We arrived in Munich without a pfennig, but decided that we could easily crash the Olympic village, built for the upcoming games, which had only just been completed. We climbed over a couple of fences and a brick wall, and squatted in the Olympic village for a few days.

I played at some of the Munich folk clubs, raising a few deutschmark, and every night we'd go out raising hell all over Munich and then scramble back over the walls of the village. I became so attached to the place that I was shocked when I saw news footage of the terrorists at the Munich Olympics. I'd had a similar experience back in London, when the sandwich shop I frequented each day, opposite the Old Bailey, was blown to smithereens by the IRA. Chilling experiences both.

I met Dieter Heisig at Kinney Records, simply by looking up the company in the phone book. Kinney was the forerunner of Warner Brothers, and later WEA Records. I played Dieter some of my songs and he began talking seriously about a deal with the label. I couldn't wait to get back to Berlin, knock the band into shape and start recording proper demos, do photo shoots, the works. This was all very exciting.

I returned to Berlin and got down to some serious writing, while Volker and I began planning our future career moves—we had that much confidence in Dieter Heisig.

'We need the very best equipment,' Volker said, so along with Fame we decided to drive to London in a Kombi van and buy second-hand Marshall amplifiers and any other necessary gear. Now that I had proper Berlin citizenship, I could enter the UK without any hassles. Two people I knew in London, Mick and Graham, agreed to put us up for a few days.

We drove via Calais in northern France and arrived on Mick and Graham's doorstep late one afternoon. They were both pissed as usual, and began making tasteless remarks about the obvious—Germans, the war, blah, blah, blah. This overt nationalism struck me very hard. I was shocked. The only thing that was vaguely amusing was Mick and Graham's insistence on watching *Hogan's Heroes* and stupidly rolling about, killing themselves laughing. We got the hell out of there, Mick and Graham howling with laughter at our backs. Volker was distraught. His father, from whom he was estranged, had been a colonel in the Wehrmacht, which was the German military, not the Nazi Party.

Our couple of days in England were absolutely bloody miserable. I was staggered at the level of hatred to which these twenty-year-old Germans were subjected. When we asked for directions in a village street, a parody of the archetypal British squire went into a rage upon hearing Fame's accent and beat the crap out of our borrowed Kombi with his walking stick. We bought our Marshall amps and headed back to Berlin posthaste.

Back in Berlin I befriended a guitarist from Spandau called Siegfried 'Siggi' Albrecht. He's still to this day one of the better guitarists I have ever played with. But because he came from a rough working-class background, he and Fame—a snooty upper-class prat—were at each other from the moment they met. And Siggi was not only dealing LSD, much to Volker's disgust, but also dropping multiple trips every day. Yet the acid seemed to have virtually no effect on him; he could function extremely well.

Siggi wasn't long for the band but I maintained a friendship with him deep into the 1970s, until he moved to England.

I was endlessly fascinated by the strange assortment of men Gisela dragged home. At thirty-something she was still elegant and beautiful, as befitting a top European model, and brilliant, but she was also extremely neurotic. She played mind games ad nauseam, especially with Volker, who'd been her lover.

Gisela's bedroom was decked out like the boudoir of silent film goddess Theda Bara—there was a huge white rug that could have been skinned off a polar bear, and her equally fluffy white Persian cat, which would glare at you with sinister eyes. Gisela's bed was a modern twist on the decor in a Valentino movie. She made several attempts to seduce me; she'd try and initiate things by masturbating the cat in front of me. The atmosphere in her chamber became a bit like that of a witches' den. Gisela unnerved me: she had strange hypnotic eyes, and a deep, almost masculine voice.

Her charades were designed mainly to undo Volker, so when she realised the depth of the friendship between Volker and me, Gisela began a bizarre campaign. She talked to me constantly and bluntly about sex, and became aggressive in her advances to me. She'd wander into my tiny bedroom, naked, and try to hop under the sheets with me.

As I was fiercely loyal to Volker, Gisela's behaviour became increasingly bizarre. She began bringing home US marines; they'd smoke copious amounts of opium in her bedroom and fuck their brains out very loudly, all night long.

Volker was starting to crack; he was drinking heavily, stumbling into alcoholism. One night Volker and I arrived home drunk again, but Gisela had changed the lock on the front door. We caused such a ruckus that she made the mistake of coming to the door and opening it slightly. Volker pounced and threw her outside. Like two giggling schoolboys, we leaned against the heavy wooden door, laughing. The next moment: 'THUD!' 'CRASH!' 'BANG!' Gisela, in a psychopathic frenzy, had returned with an axe and was hacking the front door to pieces. She actually managed to hack the door down and then terrorised us for the better part of an hour, chasing us around the flat with the axe.

Gisela eventually collapsed from exhaustion; Volker and I threw a few things together and ran.

Sadly, we never did sort things out; that was the sordid end to my time in Klausenerplatz. No more picturesque markets in the square every Tuesday, walks in the grounds of Charlottenburg Palace or riding my yellow bike across the cobblestones in the nearby streets. No more hanging out with all the cool dudes in the neighbourhood.

Although Georgie and Sabine owned their luxurious house in Wannsee, Berlin's most exclusive address, they had decided to spend most of their time in New York, leaving the furnished house unoccupied. Volker had moved in with a girl called Andrea (who was to become his wife), and so I lived alone in the big old mansion in Wannsee, at the end of the Berlin train line.

I entered an entirely different world. This was perhaps the beginning of my nightclubbing career, a lifestyle I embraced for about the next twenty years. There were many hip clubs in the centre of Berlin, mainly on Ku'damm, and I became a bit of a fixture. I was lonely at Wannsee, so I'd stay in the nightclubs until 6 or 7 a.m.—I became one of the vampires.

I started hanging out with Siggi again; being one of the local heroes, he introduced me to all the best girls, including Inge, who became my 'Prussian Blue'.

To me, Inge was simply the best-looking girl in Berlin: she had cool blue eyes, strawberry blonde hair—she was oh so Germanic. She was also neurotic. Consequently, we had quite a tempestuous relationship. This was good and bad. The good part was the crazy, passionate lovemaking in the house at Wannsee, where we'd indulge ourselves for days on end. The bad part was my jealousy of all her admirers, and her thing for morphine, then the drug of the ultra hip.

I watched her best friend Lucia, also a beautiful girl, sink into the dark world of morphine addiction: she developed sallow, sunken facial features, exuded nothing but misery and deep depression, and the track marks on her arms became abscessed and ugly. One night I nursed Lucia in my arms for ages at the back of a nightclub. Later that night they found her dead. I wrote the song 'Burning Ships'—which made my *Prussian Blue* album—as an obituary of profound sadness for Lucia.

I had an interesting creative life in Berlin; it's where I learnt to be musically schizoid. I'll always fiercely defend this quality of my musical career. At one end of the spectrum, I was playing with Fame, Burghard and often Siggi and Michael Hoenig, making weird experimental music, complete with Stockhausen sound effects. The music became a hybrid bastard of Pink Floyd—well, kinda sorta.

But my real passion lay more with singer-songwriters like James Taylor and Neil Young, as well as Bob Dylan and The Band. Siggi was easily the most proficient musician among us, and he became besotted with David Crosby's songs, written with the most amazing guitar tunings, derived from Appalachian Mountain folklore. For Siggi and me, being a world away, this just seemed so exotic.

We used to pull reasonable crowds by default, because there were virtually no original bands in Berlin at that time. Inga Rumpf, a sensational singer with the timbre of Renée Geyer, but much rockier, used to come down from Hamburg, and locals Tangerine Dream would play the occasional concert at the university, but that was about it. We went to see Frank Zappa at Deutschlandhalle, a venue much like Sydney's Hordern Pavilion; that was a rare treat. The Germans loved Zappa, Leonard Cohen and American guitarist J.J. Cale—figure that one out!

I also befriended two American draft resisters in exile in Berlin. Both were immensely talented musicians, and played solo around the folk clubs. They lived a curious life, almost invisible, just in case the US government tried to hunt them down. They feared one day being caught and sent off to the killing fields of Vietnam. There were so many weird and wonderful people like this living in Berlin in 1970. I guess there was a little of that *Casablanca* quality to the place.

Wannsee, being the most exclusive area of Berlin, was an incongruous locale for a penniless hippie. Across the road lived a bearded intellectual called Edgar, who professed to be a traditional Maoist, but was the heir to a successful business. Edgar was delightful, as was his brother Michael and Michael's girlfriend, who went by the name 'Congo'. I became very fond of these three, as eccentric as they sometimes were. Congo once slept for over a week; this was just her way of escaping from the world. She'd performed this Rumpelstiltskin act a number of times before.

I was turning a little maudlin, and was getting further and further into the netherworld of clubbing and binge drinking. The Who had just released the song 'Baba O'Riley' and I was spending my nights dancing to it at Dschungel—a nightclub recently immortalised by David Bowie in his song 'Where Are We Now'. I'd end up on the morning train with the factory workers drinking their early morning schnapps. This experience directly inspired my songs 'Factory Life' and 'Poor Man's Saviour'.

I tried hard to maintain our relationship with Dieter Heisig at Kinney Records, but in 1972 Germany didn't rate much of a mention on the international music scene. We'd encountered problems because we'd chosen the name Sopwith Camel for our band, and were promptly threatened with legal action by a big American band who had beaten us to it. Bloody awful name, anyway!

After so many years as a defiant expat, I suddenly started getting homesick. I was reading the Australian newspapers at the British Consulate, and became enamoured with this iconic political giant named Gough Whitlam. I'd lived in self-imposed exile for several years because the Australia of my youth had been a cultural wasteland. I was becoming increasingly excited about Gough Whitlam's brave new Australia. He really seemed to be hauling the place out of the dark ages.

I decided to return to London for Christmas, to be with Lois and all my English friends. I needed to talk to Lois about going home. She was living down in Kent; the snow, the house with the bay windows and the hazy streetlights in the dense darkness of an English twilight made it all look like a fairytale. I was having such a wonderful time I was tempted to give London one last shot. However, Lois thought that we should return to Australia. I headed home to Berlin to agonise over this.

I can't remember what went wrong, but I was arrested at Dover and hauled off for deportation. I remember some pig of a customs officer completely dismantled my Gibson and left it in several pieces on the bench. My prized guitar! By now I'd had a gutful.

I was thrown into the brig of the cross-channel ferry with an aristocratic Austrian girl and we sailed for Calais. Oddly, this became the most romantic adventure of my life. There is something about being in a situation like this with a beautiful foreign girl—again, it's very *Casablanca*. We started making love deep in the hold of the ferry and reached Calais in the middle of the night.

I'd phoned Volker about my dilemma, and he managed to leave a prepaid ticket for me at the station. I boarded the train with the Austrian princess (well, she was a princess to me), and we made love all the way to Marseilles. There was heavy snow that year, so the whole train was frosted over and had a very Agatha Christie feel to it. We parted ways in the south of France, pledging undying love.

I suddenly felt very alone. My Berlin residency and work permit had expired—I was a stateless refugee. The train to Germany was almost deserted. My precious guitar, my only possession, was in pieces. The Austrian girl had given me enough money for just a day or two. The train was hurtling through East Germany, the point furthest from Australia. There was a snowstorm raging; it must have been minus 30 degrees outside.

We approached the West Berlin border and I heard the East German border police board the train. They were dressed in uniforms that bore an uncanny resemblance to the old SS outfits, and came stomping down the corridor of the train in their jackboots, shouting. I really believed that this was it for me, the end of the road. The man in charge barged into my compartment.

'Show me your papers!' he barked at me in guttural German. He was a real bastard. It was like being interrogated by the Gestapo.

I decided to play the dumb Aussie abroad.

'I can't understand you,' I said. 'What are you saying?'

But he was no fool; he could see by my papers that I'd lived in Berlin for two years. Just when I thought I was about to be hauled off to Siberia forever, he exploded into laughter, speaking in a strong Aussie accent: 'You dumb bastard—yer fucked, aren't ya?'

I was in disbelief but persisted with my dumb Aussie act.

'Cut the crap, arsehole,' he said. 'Mate, yer up shitcreek in a barbed wire canoe without paddles. No fuckin' residency papers, eh?'

I found out that while he was born in Dresden, his family had emigrated to Moorabbin, where he'd lived for fifteen years. He spoke English with a perfect Melburnian accent. Crazy.

'Yer so fuckin' lucky you got me, arsehole. C'mon, I'll take yer into the office and give you new papers, yer fuckwit.'

This was one of the most bizarre experiences of my life. I was still reeling as he stamped my papers for another twelve months.

When I arrived back in Berlin, Volker was totally besotted with Andrea and their courtship had no place for me; three really was a crowd. Georg and Sabine remained in New York City. Siggi was now a part of a fairly heavy drug scene. I must say, this period of my life turned me off the culture of hard drugs.

Clearly, it was time for me to leave. Lois met me in Amsterdam, and we set sail on P & O's *Oriana*, bound for the great south land. I'm glad I returned by ship: I revisited the Canary Islands, and Dakar on the westernmost tip of Africa.

I'll be forever grateful that I was fortunate enough to have lived through those remarkable times in Europe. Having written it all down, it hardly seems real at all.

6

'And I've got this feeling in my heart,
That it's time to raise the blinds and
change the scene'

Down The Road

Lois and I arrived back in Australia in 1972 and for a time I moved in with her family in Chatswood. They were lovely people, but I needed my independence and began planning my next move. Alas, my long hair prohibited me from finding a job. This was a real culture shock; I had forgotten about Robert Menzies' ultra conservative Australia. It was like a giant step back in time. The good news was that I had returned just a little too early. The influence of Whitlam was already quite strong; soon enough, there was no better place to live in the world than Australia.

One day, while on a job hunt, I passed the Phonogram Records offices in Oxford Street, Darlinghurst. I always carried a demo cassette of songs in my back pocket.

'Why not?' I figured, and went inside.

I asked to see their A&R man (as in artist and repertoire, the person who signs new talent), and was ushered into the office of a guy who listened to about three of my songs and immediately produced a record contract.

'Take it home and read it,' he suggested. 'If you like it, come back tomorrow and we'll sign a three-year deal.'

I was flabbergasted. I rode the train to Chatswood in a state of shock.

Despite the fact that I didn't have a clue what I was doing, and had no legal advice, I returned the next day and signed the contract.

Soon after, in mid-1972, I walked into the Sydney offices of music publisher Essex Music. There I met John Brommell, whose title was 'professional manager'—essentially, he was the liaison between a songwriter and the administrator of their songs. A pretty damned essential person, especially as I was on my way to 'turning pro'.

'Brom', who passed away in 2013 as I was writing this book, was one of the few music industry heavies who demonstrated an understanding and compassion towards local musicians. John had been a drummer in a successful group called The Cicadas; I think that explains a lot. The man was a legend. He also listened to my tape and loved it. He asked me about the Phonogram deal.

'Here's what we'll do,' an angry Brom told me. 'You should sign with us at Essex and then I'll get you out of this shitty deal with Phonogram.'

I was of course, very confused. I didn't quite know what to do or who to believe. John's boss, Barry Kimberly, scoffed at the idea of any sort of advance payment for me. John was so pissed off that he pulled $200 out of his own pocket.

'Here,' he insisted, 'take this.'

There was something incredibly charming about this great big ocker. I wanted to trust him, and thank Christ I did! Against his boss's wishes, John signed me to a two-year deal with Essex—and dealt with the Phonogram 'problem'.

'If Phonogram has any objections,' John said down the phone, 'then go ahead and sue us. Bye bye!'

John set up an appointment to see David Sinclair and record producer Richard Batchens at Festival Records, the label for such successful acts as Johnny O'Keefe and the Bee Gees. Billy Thorpe and pop stars Sherbet recorded for Infinity Records, part of the Festival empire. Sinclair and Batchens were a right couple of desperados. I was quite shocked at how much they were drinking when we met. I guess this was the beginning of my two decades of decadence.

We went to the corner pub near Festival HQ, which they'd christened the 'Pyrmont Hilton'. They ridiculed me for being a wimp, but there was no way I could keep up with their alcohol intake. I was very nervous, and didn't want to get drunk. I was starting to take my career very seriously and didn't want to screw up.

For the second time in recent history, I was presented with a recording contract, and told to have a read before signing it. I still have that contract; looking back, Festival must have killed themselves laughing at the demands I eventually made. There is nothing in that contract about royalty payments or accounting or anything technical. I insisted on weird abstractions like spelling out the rules of play between myself and the producer, and vetoing who could and could not play on my records. Nothing about money. They signed off on my demands swiftly—and that was that. A record deal.

The stress on Richard Batchens must have been bloody awful; it was usually a terse environment in the studio. Every album I did with him—from 1973's *Prussian Blue* to 1977's *Goodbye Tiger*—felt like being locked in a bunker with a lot of very suspect bits of artillery. Whenever a bomb went off, it produced probably the fieriest sessions in the history of Australian recording.

I signed the Festival contract mainly because of the utter disappointment I felt when the Kinney deal fell through in Munich. I wasn't going to muck around for another five years. As we all know, sometimes this is as good as it gets; I guess fate and destiny have a way of forcing your hand. To be fair, however, in 1972 Festival was probably the best company around. The staff was all getting on a bit, having been a major force in the early rock'n'roll days of Johnny O'Keefe. The building in Pyrmont, especially the studio, felt a bit dated—even the decor resembled some old black and white movie from the 1950s.

There's been a myth that I had an acrimonious relationship with Festival but this was simply not true. What happened was that the 'powers that used to be' at Festival robbed me of several chances of international success, which I'll get to in time. But the general staff at Festival were a wonderful bunch of loonies.

❖

Sydney was rife with acoustic folk clubs in 1972, and I forced myself to perform as much as possible. This type of performance was totally different to playing in a loud rock band. It's like standing naked in Wynyard railway station at peak hour; I was terrified.

There was a club in the cellar of the YMCA in Oxford Street, called PACT Folk. This is where I first met many of the local 'folkies' like Mike McLelland, Terry Hannigan and John J. Francis. Music identity Glenn A. Baker was managing an act called Paul Pulati; Glenn promoted folk concerts called 'Woodsmoke and Oranges'. There was a tremendous sense of camaraderie at these gigs, and because I still looked a bit of a kid, the others watched out for me.

In order to cope with my stage fright, I used to drink way too much. Unfortunately my drinking was about as skilful as my finger picking on the guitar; most gigs ended up a mess. The Sydney folk scene was a bit of a fantasy, really; it was like being transported to a faux Greenwich Village in the 1960s.

I hung out with Terry Hannigan and sometimes crashed at his place in Chippendale. We'd drink a lot and sit around his kitchen singing each other's songs, behaving like textbook beatniks. Terry had this unnerving habit: he'd fix you with a fiendish look when he'd sing his songs, staring right into your eyes. It was really off-putting. I'd soon meet the singer Jeff St John, who went on to have his own stellar career; he had a similar trait. I understood that this intensity was born of their passionate obsession with their music, but it didn't make it any less irritating.

Sydney was thriving with the most weird and wonderful eccentrics. Singers Wendy Saddington and Leo de Castro—who recorded the first version of 'Heading in the Right Direction', later a big hit for Renée Geyer—were two of the most colourful characters on the local scene.

I remember more about Wendy herself than I do of her music. I was sent around to her 'pad' in Paddington to play some of my songs—her presence is something I'll never forget. Her little abode seemed almost like a gypsy caravan, very cluttered and dark with lots of fascinating bric-a-brac scattered around. Without seeming unkind, she reminded me a little of Rosaleen Norton, the 'witch of Kings Cross', an artist and occultist. Wendy really had a startling presence.

Leo was not just eccentric, and by his own admission quite crazy, he also had a volatile temperament—the guy could be like a naked flame near an LP gas tanker. I say this affectionately, because Leo really is a very warm human being, and one hell of a singer. There's much talk nowadays of 'emotional quota' and, believe me, Leo had excessive 'EQ'. He would regularly appear at my gigs, very intoxicated, and we'd duet on the J.J. Cale song 'Magnolia' and would continue singing and playing until they were packing the bar stools on top of the beer-sodden tables.

The hippest venue in town was the Kirk Gallery, a derelict church in Surry Hills that had been transformed into a trendy folk club. The club played a big part in my early attempts at becoming a serious performer. I'd realised that artificial stimuli were counterproductive to my performance, so I was trying to get on stage sober and overcome my dreadful stage fright. This was good because I remember a lot more about the Kirk Gallery days than some other periods of my life and career!

There was a very strong and warm camaraderie between artist and audience. The artists' room out the back was frequented by fantastic inner city hippie girls, all dressed in their 'op shop' hand me downs—they were as gentle and flowing as pixies in a children's book. The usual performers at the Kirk were from a rather small clique who played various venues in Balmain and the Cross—there was a little folk circuit all within a 20-kilometre radius.

However, I was restless. I didn't want to be a folkie. I wanted to be a rock singer. I can't remember who sent me to audition for a jazz/rock band called Sun, but the audition was held in the legendary Yellow House in Potts Point, owned by renowned Sydney artist Martin Sharp and frequented by other celebrated artists. It was early 1973 and Sun were about to part ways with their singer, a woman called Renée Geyer, so somebody came up with this cockamamie idea that I should replace her. I confidently bullshitted my way through a bit of John Coltrane and Ornette Coleman—both jazz greats—and tried to sing like a hybrid of rock-blues growler Captain Beefheart and jazzman Leontopolis Thomas. Amazingly, I got the gig.

Sun had an album with RCA records and were quite well known; they had aspirations of becoming some kind of Oz jazz all-stars. I played lots of gigs with Sun over the next few months—proof that I can sometimes fool all of the people all of the time. We were quite big on the uni scene and to be fair, there was a certain validity to our music; in a 'naive painter' sense there were always some great creative ideas flying about when we played. But this was not my niche. I knew I had to get a rock'n'roll band of my own and hit the road.

Still *sans* band, I was introduced to established industry figures like Billy Thorpe and promoter Michael Chugg and started playing solo. In 1973 I played some supports to Thorpe and his band the Aztecs, and also one of the big pop acts of the day. 'Thorpey' and his fans intimidated the hell out of me, but it probably worked in my favour; the concerts became classic 'David and Goliath' scenarios.

I played alone on a beaten up acoustic guitar, and was so nervous I'd pee about twenty times before stage time. I couldn't drink booze for fear of making an ass of myself, so my stage fright was at its worst. But I guess because I had very long, flowing hair and a gentle persona, the little girls loved me—or at least took pity on me. The audience knew what was waiting, anyway: Thorpey and the band's stack of amplifiers that looked like the Berlin Wall. Billy played louder than any other human being before him (or after him for that matter). I always felt for the Aztecs—they looked like they were in the most excruciating agony from this gargantuan wall of sound. But the Aztecs weren't just brash, they were the wildest musos I'd ever encountered. (Seriously, they make today's pussy rock stars seem like bank tellers.)

I'll never forget the last night of that tour. The poor sucker who'd promoted the tour attempted to impress Billy and the band with a lavish spread. Billy and the Aztecs stormed into the room and proceeded to trash *everything*: the furniture, the food, the booze, the carpet—they even had a food fight with some innocent bystanders. It was wild.

As for the big pop band tour, it reached a colourful crescendo on the fifteenth floor of the Crest Hotel in Brisbane. I'd been hanging around the fringes of their legion of groupies, but never really wanted to join in the fun. In Brisbane I returned to my room to find a rather pretty young girl camped on my doorstep. For some reason, I decided to let her into my room, and she smoked a joint—which I found rather off-putting. I suppose the memory of the drug bust in London a couple of years before still made me paranoid about the police.

'Okay,' I told her, 'time to go,' but to no avail. She stripped stark naked and jumped into my bed.

'I'm not going anywhere,' she insisted.

The band, who were staying on the same floor, returned around midnight and were raising hell. Now I was getting extra paranoid about a drug bust. I peeked out my door and looked down the hall in the direction of all the noise. The band had their doors wide open and I could see that there were a number of girls in various states of undress—I could also see a range of drugs being handed out.

I freaked. I had a pot-smoking hippie girl in my bed and the party down the hall just got louder and louder, way out of control. In the early hours of the morning, from behind my locked door, I heard an entourage of uniformed police heading towards the band's rooms. Muffled arguments were conducted behind the closed doors, and I was sure the local coppers would discover the details of my altercation with the British drug squad and off to jail I would go.

The muffled voices ceased; silence returned to the fifteenth floor. I had my ear to the door, but heard nothing more and went to bed for what remained of a night of restless sleep with my pot-smoking groupie. I was up reasonably early, kissed her bye bye and headed downstairs for my free breakfast. A short time later, a member of the band's entourage joined me at my table.

'What the fuck happened last night?' I asked with great trepidation.

'Whaddya mean, what happened last night?' he asked me.

I shut up and ate my breakfast.

7

'And now I'm here
Waiting for your telephone call,
With my head on the floor'

Last Train to Marseilles

During the first half of the 1970s I wrote prolifically; I really had the 'hunger'. Much of my time was spent in a very decrepit flat overlooking William Street, Kings Cross, the perfect spot for an angst-ridden young songwriter. 'I Wanna Be a Survivor' was written there, and the song still carries the musty odour of that old flat.

I played everything onto a cheap cassette player, and was still enough of a vampire to sit up until dawn every night, writing songs, then sleep until 2 p.m. The first song of mine to be regarded as having any commercial potential was 'Last Train to Marseilles', about my Austrian princess. It was also written in this dingy flat.

Richard Batchens and I commenced pre-production on the song and he enlisted the legendary 'Red' McKelvie as a creative partner on the production. I was absolutely in awe of Red. He'd led a famous Australian country-rock band called Flying Circus, who'd had hit singles in Australia (including the song 'Hayride') and achieved great success in

Australia and Canada. Red was as colourful a character as I'd met.

Not only was Red red-headed but he also sported a red Colonel Custer moustache. He'd get really drunk with beer foam all over his moustache, and wax lyrical about interstate truckers, or certain chapters of the Hell's Angels who were good buddies of his. When I discovered he'd been having an interesting sexual liaison with the secretary of one of Festival Records chief execs, I had an anxiety attack, believing that, were he found out, it could spell a very premature end to my recording career. However, I was soon to learn that the entire Australian record industry was rife with rampant lasciviousness.

Red was a hard taskmaster in the studio, whose philosophy was 'a fair day's work for a fair day's dollar'. He was always at loggerheads with the corporate types at Festival, but was revered as much as he was feared. There had simply never been a better guitar player in Australia, even if his contribution to the local industry has been largely overlooked.

Red had all the dexterity, craftmanship and technique necessary for transforming my songs into good records. He took control of 'Last Train to Marseilles' and crafted it into a country-pop masterwork. Over the next few years, Red and I got better and better together—my first hit, 1975's 'Girls on the Avenue', was probably our finest achievement.

We tried to fight the good fight, but the industry in the 1970s was awash with boozing and long lunches; it's a miracle any great art was able to surface at all. I was always concerned for Red's welfare; one minute he'd simply be agitated and then he'd explode into a rage. After tough days in Festival's studios, Red would coerce me to walk all the way home from Pyrmont to Bondi, where I had moved after Kings Cross, a distance of about 15 kilometres, at 4 a.m.

'Otherwise,' Red told me, 'I'll never get to sleep.'

The recording of my *Prussian Blue* album was a necessary exercise in producer fascism. I had had not one iota of studio experience and needed a pedantic taskmaster like Richard Batchens; he put me through a crash course in studio discipline. Session musos were hired in a rather haphazard fashion, which regrettably scarred some of my old songs for life.

Each day was a constant tussle between Richard and myself. I'd be lobbying for the hip rock musicians like Kevin Borich and the La De Das or Country Radio (and later, the Dingoes). Batchens, however, would usually win out and I'd be stuck with staid session musicians who earned their living from TV tonight shows and music jingles.

Yet I have no real regrets about this; it gave me a solid start in my professional recording career. At least these session men had excellent formal backgrounds and really knew their stuff, technically speaking. I was an ignoramus, trying his best. I used to have terrible anxiety attacks playing guitar among a group of grumpy, impatient old session musicians. Fortunately, I was able to keep up with them.

The music industry introduced me to binge drinking; it's the one aspect of my life I've found singularly unappealing. The 'powers that be' in the music industry would hang out at a strange place on Sydney's lower north shore called the 729 Club. It was more speakeasy than legitimate club, and it was here I learned some truths about the music industry. I best not single anyone out, because I cannot think of *anyone* in this business who is without sin, myself included. And many of these people became friends. I was new to the industry and unprepared for all this. My songs were like children to me; I found these drunken orgies—and the reality of the business I was entering—very off-putting.

Industry politics would come to play such a significant role in my story and impact greatly on the lives of the people I was close to. I learned very early just how distracting and obstructive these politics could be to my creative flow. I saw this in Red McKelvie, too. It seemed to me that Red had a great talent that was being suffocated, although I was determined to keep his spirit buoyant. Fortunately, I was still young enough to be able to rise above these conflicts, at least for the time being.

As Festival's in-house producer, Richard Batchens had power, which he wielded relentlessly in the studio. Richard would attempt to dictate all Red's guitar lines by humming them, or worse still, singing what he heard in his head. To talented musicians this was hell. The worse thing was that Richard's musical ideas were sometimes out of date; they belonged to the bad ol' days of Tin Pan Alley.

The release of *Prussian Blue* in November 1973 marked the start of my real career. This was when I first learned that glowing critical acclaim for your work doesn't necessarily translate to commercial success. I still can't fathom the exact reason for this, but would guess it's probably because rock critics are often not in tune with the public. But as I said, I'm not exactly sure how the process works. All I can tell you is that *Prussian Blue* received rave reviews—and consequently 'stiffed'. 'Last Train to Marseilles' received a little airplay, mainly in New South Wales, but that was about it.

I might have been poor, but I began to enjoy life to the full. I coerced Red into forming a band with me, and we started a residency at French's Wine Bar on the notorious Oxford Street in Darlinghurst. It seemed to only take two or three gigs and suddenly we were flavour of the month, packing in the crowds, even though we couldn't afford a PA.

Red and I had a fluid roster of different drummers and bass players, but Englishman Brian Bethell was probably our main bassist, Dave Ovenden our first-choice drummer.

In the summertime, the hippies would cram into French's and spill out onto the footpath all the way down Oxford Street. By now I was a seasoned drinker and would knock back countless Black Russians (Strongbow cider with a dark mixer) as I played, and the audience would sway along to my songs. It really looked like a scene from a Toulouse-Lautrec painting.

I slept with a number of girls during this time, but unlike my ocker mates, I always fell in love. I fell hard for one of the barmaids from French's. Predictably, I ended up moving in with her, into a lovely little bedsit in Bondi. Her brother would bring her gifts of marijuana, and we enjoyed wine, sex and music, taken in that order. My songwriting was developing nicely; I had a wealth of material and inspiration to draw from.

I worked with a New York native, a guitarist named Roy. He was married to a stunning woman from New Mexico called Linda, who looked like a mix of Joni Mitchell and Joan Baez. They had moved to Australia as two hippie refugees; when I met them they were living in Annandale in Sydney's inner west, but they needed to be out in the country, not battling the cockroaches in a grotty dump. Roy and Linda and their young son moved up to Byron Bay, searching for idyllic respite.

I wrote 'Blue Bay Blues' about these wonderful idealists; to this day it's one of my most requested songs, so I guess many people can relate. (I changed Linda's name to 'Janie' in the song; I felt they deserved some privacy.) I continued to keep in touch with them as they drifted in and out of my life.

After Roy left, I managed to put a great band together with a few of the best musicians in town. We mainly played a residency near Wollongong for many months; not only did it pay the rent, but we built up a staunchly loyal following on the NSW South Coast, which continues today.

We played to probably 300 to 400 people each night. The guy who owned the restaurant/wine bar was a racing car driver in his spare time and used to drive me back to Sydney at alarming speeds, at all hours. Sometimes we'd play a few nights in a row, and would stay in a nice house overlooking the ocean. It was a great escape from the pace of Sydney.

Back in Sydney, French's had become established as the premier venue for credible rock and blues music. Every night the joint was jumping, packed to the rafters with drunken music lovers. Locals the Foreday Riders belted out the best blues this side of Chicago, and Glyn Mason's band Home played the finest swamp rock outside of Muscle Shoals, the legendary studio in Alabama.

I was having the time of my life hanging out with the many beautiful girls who frequented the place and getting blind drunk with my mates. And it was at French's where perhaps my best-known song came to life.

8

'But don't you slip – don't you slip
in love with the girls on the avenue'

Girls on the Avenue

At the time my best mate was Colin Vercoe, a manager for Festival's music publishing department. We rented a house in Rose Bay. After the poor sales on *Prussian Blue*, Festival had given me the classic ultimatum: 'Come up with a hit single or be damned!' In other words, no hit and they'd drop me from the label.

Colin was girl crazy and had the largest collection of *Penthouse* magazines I had ever seen. All he could think about was girls and music (in that order). One balmy summer evening in 1975, Colin and I were sitting in the front window of French's, gazing wistfully at the many pretty girls strolling down Oxford Street.

Our conversation was adolescent and chauvinistic; we could think of nothing else than trying to get laid. But Colin was the A&R man for Festival's publishing company, and he laid on me the most impassioned rave about making this one important compromise with the bosses at Festival Records.

'You can write a hit,' he told me.

We made our drunken way home to Rose Bay, first stocking up at a liquor store. Colin retired to his room, and I sat up all night with my guitar and tape deck. I had music in my head and I was determined to get this song out. I continued drinking quite heavily. We lived in the next street along from The Avenue, Rose Bay, and I had been having carnal thoughts about the 'girls on the avenue'.

Colin and I lived on Chaleyer Street in Rose Bay, and the next street along was called—you guessed it—The Avenue. Just around the corner, about halfway up The Avenue, a number of very pretty girls shared a house together. Colin and I were always plotting how we could chat them up one day. As corny as it sounds, that is exactly what the song is about. 'Girls on The Avenue' (Rose Bay). Get it?

Abuse of any drug, especially alcohol, creates this chaos in your head, and if you read the lyrics to 'Girls on the Avenue' you'll notice that my train of thought gets derailed, but the poetic metaphors were coming thick and fast. (I was horrified a year or so later when a lobby group of hookers came to my gig in Adelaide and treated me like some revolutionary poet. It took me a while to understand how anybody could read allusions to prostitutes in my song. However precious I may have been, I was eventually converted when I started receiving handsome royalties for 'Girls on the Avenue'.)

But I'm getting ahead of myself. Colin woke up in the morning to the strains of me playing 'Girls on the Avenue'. He was so enthralled that he started driving me nuts. That day Colin went to work and started his 'Girls' campaign. Unfortunately, his wild enthusiasm worked against us in a perverse sort of way.

You see, some record company people have a phobia about anything that may have eluded them; they need a sense of ownership. Festival seemed determined to hate my song and with each A&R meeting they vetoed 'Girls' on the grounds that the arrangement was haphazard and the song didn't make sense. Colin grew increasingly agitated. I have to mention, too, that Festival had just passed up the chance to grab the catalogue of up-and-comer Bruce Springsteen, soon to be a major star, for all of $200, so their radar way way off.

Richard Batchens stood by me and agreed to record the song on Festival's brand new, cutting-edge 24-track console. We recorded no fewer than seventeen guitar tracks on 'Girls on the Avenue', way more than the standard. We went a little crazy.

Richard set out to become Australia's answer to Phil Spector, the master of 'The Wall of Sound', and he was not mucking around. We had embarked on what I think was perhaps the most arduous recording exercise undertaken by anyone in this country. Every note, every beat on that recording is as close to perfect as we could hope without using any studio tricks. Richard would keep me in the studio for sixteen, seventeen hours a day, 'doubling' guitar tracks mercilessly. I would sometimes have to tune my guitar for hours before he would even consent to hitting 'record'.

The recording sessions never seemed to end; after the seventeen guitar tracks, Richard had me doing vocal backings ad nauseam, stacking harmony upon harmony until he had a wall of my voices to play with when he came to 'mix' the record. Tony Ansell, who played on all my early records, was a godsend; he was like a human keyboard sampler. I'd sing abstract ideas at Tony and he would interpret exactly what I wanted, much of it inspired by Al Kooper's keyboard work on early Bob Dylan recordings, including 'Like a Rolling Stone'.

I must admit that while I thought I might lose my mind making 'Girls', its quality is proof that we could make records the equal of anyone in the world. Forty years later, if you're a lover of analogue recordings and long for that 'seventies sound', it's better than many records made today.

Unfortunately, Festival's A&R committee still couldn't hear it. Dismayed, Richard, Colin and I went on some shocking drinking binges. To make matters worse, I had set a Banjo Paterson poem to music, and had approached a couple of the Dingoes, a great local country-rock band, and some members of Country Radio to record it with me. It was nice enough, and the Dingoes were great players; I figured it would have been a solid album track. But the A&R committee, in all their wisdom, decided that this was going to be a huge hit. They scheduled my next release: 'Travelling Down the Castlereagh' as the *single*, with 'Girls on the Avenue' as the B-side.

Colin had had enough. He'd been offered a job at the new Sydney radio station 2JJ, as their first music programmer, which he was agonising over. Now, however, he had his mind made up for him. He ambushed an A&R meeting in Festival's boardroom, demanding to know why they continued to reject 'Girls on the Avenue'.

'There's no chorus,' he was told. 'It's not strong enough.'

Colin exploded and put his fist right through one of the plywood panels in the boardroom.

'I fucking quit!' he yelled.

A week or two later, Colin took the Double J job. I wasn't receiving much airplay on 'Travelling Down the Castlereagh', but heard a few upbeat comments about 'Girls on the Avenue'. Because Colin had been given carte blanche by his new bosses, he took it upon himself to play 'Girls on the Avenue' relentlessly. In those first weeks of transmission, *everybody* was listening to the new radio station—suddenly established pop stations such as 2SM in Sydney and Melbourne's 3XY started to play 'Girls', putting it into 'high rotation'.

Everything happened so fast, as it does in pop music. Much to Festival's chagrin, 'Girls on the Avenue' zoomed to the top of the singles charts in early 1975—not bad for a B-side! (The album of the same name followed in April and stayed on the charts for several months.) I needed to get a band together and assembled the rhythm section from the 'Girls' recording sessions—Dave Ovenden on drums and Brian Bethell on bass—and my guru, Red, on guitar. I went from unknown hippie folk singer to pop star overnight; I flew in planes for the first time in my life, and stayed in all the nice hotels.

Soon after, the band and I were playing at the notorious Station Hotel in Melbourne's Prahran, ground zero for AC/DC. We were hot—as was the weather—and the place was packed. A couple of the guys from the Dingoes got up on stage with us, and the crowd went troppo. A few inebriated girls jumped up on stage and the dudes in the audience (a peculiar mix of hippies and ockers) were chanting, 'Show us your tits!' Some of the more intrepid girls did just that and, of course, brought the house down. (I met one of these girls years later, when she was a successful TV producer. She told me that the heat and the booze drove her a little crazy that night at the Station.)

Despite my early struggles, I was fortunate that I came on the Australian scene when I did. This was the era of *Digger* and *Go-Set* magazines and the fledgling Australian *Rolling Stone*. Local music was being taken more seriously. There were great venues, including the T.F. Much Ballroom in Melbourne and the Bondi Lifesaver in Sydney, Brisbane's Cloudland Ballroom, the Marryatville in Adelaide and the Sandgroper in Perth. The bills were filled by such greats as Country Radio and Blackfeather, Spectrum and Chain.

I began developing personal relationships with some of the music writers. Colin Talbot was a fine author in his own right;

Gary Hutchison was a great (published) poet; Dave Dawson was the larrikin. It was a rich time. Further down the track, this great Australian heritage was kept alive and well by the likes of Ed St John, Toby Creswell, Glenn A. Baker and Stuart Coupe, plus photographers and artists like Graeme Webber and Ian McCausland who lived with us musicians, indulged in all our excesses and truly understood the life and the music. Graphic artists were also an integral part of the local music scene.

David N. Pepperell, a true Beat writer and simply the most flamboyant character I've ever befriended, was probably best known as 'Doctor Pepper'. He had borrowed $2000 with his mate Keith Glass and together they started a record store in Melbourne called Archie and Jugheads. David was well on his way to becoming a millionaire before he was thirty, and he was a little like Dudley Moore's character in the film *Arthur* (although some people have likened me to Arthur, too). He would work in his shop all day, then dine in expensive restaurants with an array of beautiful women, drink copious amounts of fine red wine, ingest a smorgasbord of substances and go looking for the best bands in town. Writing as Doctor Pepper, he was the most feared and loathed critic in all Australia, and a great writer, to boot. Luckily, we became good friends.

Mostly, Dr Pepper and I hung out with Mark Barnes and his wife Morag, who ran the Station Hotel. These people were real-life Kerouac characters, who'd imbibe vast quantities of substances and stay up for days, raving manifestos and opinions. Passion dripped from the walls, and insanity ran in the family. We would rant about Anaïs Nin, Bob Dylan, Pharoah Sanders, Allen Ginsberg and Sylvia Plath.

One night Pepperell was in such a drunken rage that he got into his Jaguar, revved it up and drove through the walls of the Station. On another night I kicked my girlfriend's car and hurled a brick through her window because I thought she was having an affair with someone. (I was right, by the way.) Once, while on a bender, Pepperell dropped acid, took some speed and caught a red-eye to LA. He went straight to Anaïs Nin's house and demanded that she speak with him. According to David, he ended up staying there for days.

Dr Pepper had no fear of the big pop acts of the day. His behaviour towards these bands and their record company people kept us in stitches. Pepperell revelled in singling out these sacred cows and ripping them to shreds. Everything that the record companies' marketing departments hyped, Dr Pepper would unravel in a half page in *Juke* magazine. Ditto Dave Dawson. Pepperell and Dawson were living dangerously. They spoke out loud—nay, shouted at the top of their voices—about forbidden things that were supposed to be sacrosanct. The dangerous thing about Dr Pepper is that he never had any skeletons in his closet. He was weirder than the lot of them.

❖

Back in Sydney, life was pretty great, and I was having a ball. I was still playing with Red, a strict disciplinarian who would not take crap from anyone. Red sacked Brian Bethell in the middle of playing 'Girls on the Avenue' at an RSL club—by song's end he was never seen again. We found a very young bass player in Canberra, Michael Hegerty, who replaced Bethell. Michael was to become my musical partner for fifteen years.

I'd also taken up with a manager, who'd been introduced to me by Frank Stivala, my agent. When Michael first joined my band, the musicians were only scraping by on $25 to $50 a week; we were all too poor to pay rent or buy food or drinks. Thankfully we had a plethora of fiercely loyal fans.

Michael was so naive. The manager would pay him his meagre wage, then immediately ask him to invest in the band's future—so he'd give his wage straight back to pay off band debts. Michael fell for this time after time despite Red and me lecturing him relentlessly.

By now, Red had gone as far as he could go with my band; he was simply too old to be dragged mercilessly around the country, playing as much as three times a day and driving from Perth to Brisbane.

My band became increasingly unstable; Michael was the only constant. Michael and I formed one line-up with drummer Ace Follington and spent a very debauched but pleasant couple of weeks living in a beach house at Surfers Paradise, playing a residency at the Chevron Hotel.

We had a guitarist who was moving quite large quantities of hashish, which he hid under his mother-in-law's house. The entire band was pretty bent. The guitarist made up a punishment called 'thirteen hits for the aunty mate'. This meant that if a player in the band made too many mistakes, or screwed up in some way, he'd have to take thirteen tokes on a hash joint. I was forced to endure this punishment one night and spent the gig asking Michael to guide me through all the chords to my own songs, while the audience looked on, laughing. I ended the night by stripping off most of my clothes and auctioning each item.

Frankly, I was kept afloat by the unswerving critical support I received; I always seemed to be either in the press or on the radio. Sometimes both. That's something for which I'll be forever grateful.

9

'So much dirt on the street,
it sticks to the edge of your feet'

Need a Visionary

The Richard Clapton Band had built a very solid following in Melbourne, so in 1976 we decided to relocate there. Diane had recently joined as a backing vocalist, and Tony and drummer Iain McLennan played regularly with Ross Wilson and Mike Rudd's Ariel, both of whom were Melbourne based. Six of us, including our roadie Graham, took over a one-bedroom flat in Darling Street, South Yarra. The place was ludicrously small, yet we could barely manage the rent, let alone buy food or beer. Someone would walk down to the local markets and buy as much food as we could afford (usually some vegies) and this would sustain the whole band, week in and week out. We scrounged enough work to help us survive, but it was tough.

We became industry outsiders, and were ostracised for a number of reasons. My rebellious attitude towards the corporate side of the music industry probably didn't help. We closed ranks and found solidarity with the Dingoes and Ariel and many of the other Melbourne bands.

I stumbled across a gig at the Kingston Hotel. The manager

was a huge fan of mine; he agreed to let us play there and collect money on the door; some of our girlfriends helped collect the cash from punters—at least in theory, anyway. The first gig was fantastic as a musical event and the bar filled up very fast.

I thought I was well on my way to establishing an alternative music world—the place was really jumping. Ross Wilson, Ross Hannaford and Gary Young—all members of the legendary Daddy Cool—and guys from the Dingoes and Ariel got up and played with us. The camaraderie was fantastic.

We were charging something like $5 entrance, and we figured that we'd collect a couple of grand at the door. Alas, there was no money; everyone in the room was a musician, a partner of a musician, some local industry personality or well-known ligger—so no one felt obliged to pay. The publican, who did a roaring trade, sympathised and served us a raging torrent of free beer.

We persevered, playing the Kingston once a week. Such great Melbourne bands as The Sports and Jo Jo Zep and the Falcons eventually turned the room into a legendary venue.

It was good while it lasted, a real blast—and these were some lively times. Groupies were rife, not just in Melbourne but across the entire nation, from Cairns to Fremantle. There were thousands of girls who partied very hard with well-known rock'n'roll bands out on the road 365 nights a year. Had I been more lecherous, I could have had sex with many girls. Amazing women, like the immortal Lithgow Leaper, performed astounding sexual feats with every band that came into town.

The 'gang bang' was the most common sexual practice. One or two girls would allow the whole band to penetrate every orifice; the more modest girls would take on each band member one by one—the even more polite would insist on only one band member in the room at a time.

I moved into a flat in Melbourne with a new girlfriend some days afterwards and we embarked on a wonderful voyage of sexual adventure. The weeks turned into months and she began to open up more and more; she'd even show me secret photographs. I think that this was my first foray into the Jungian 'dark side', at least sexually speaking. We both shared a propensity for barbiturates and beer, and invented highly erotic sexual games that would sometimes last for hours. I learnt that a powerful imagination is the key to eroticism.

Unfortunately, the booze could turn things violent. This is the only relationship I have been in that sometimes got a little ugly. We were both guilty of smashing up the house, the furniture and each other. However, from this quagmire emerged some of my best songs to date, which appeared on my next album, *Mainstreet Jive*, released in August 1976. Songs like 'Need a Visionary', 'Suit Yourself' and 'Kickin' the Moon Around' eclipsed anything I'd written on the *Girls on the Avenue* LP. I'll always regard *Mainstreet Jive* as my Melbourne album.

❖

While in Melbourne I became close friends with Chris Stockley from the Dingoes. He and his girlfriend Jenny lived in a large, rambling house in Kew, with various members of Ariel. The house was the scene of some of the best parties I've ever attended. The *crème de la crème* of Melbourne's music community would show up for heavy drinking and partying sessions that could sometimes continue for days. David N. Pepperell and Dave Dawson were always there, too. We all shared a predilection for the great new songwriters, people like Danny O'Keefe (whose song 'The Road' was covered by Jackson Browne), Lowell George from the band Little Feat, Randy Newman, Rickie Lee Jones and Joni Mitchell. Our huge record collections became a sort of community library. We soaked it all up, but remained insatiable.

Together we lived out this wild bohemian fantasy. The future powerbrokers of Australian music, like Michael Chugg and Frank Stivala, also lived this life to the full. Born from this hedonistic decadence was a true camaraderie, which has endured in an odd sort of way. Various artists and photographers were also in the mix.

While on the subject of hedonism, I cannot speak about the exploits of various acts first-hand, but the stories of a certain Polaroid collection of nubile nymphets in all states of sexual debauchery are not just legend, but true.

Then there was AC/DC. Their singer Bon Scott used to show up at a lot of our gigs. Initially I flattered myself that he was simply a fan. Well, that may have been true, but after a while I realised that it was actually Diane, my back-up singer, that he was even more interested in. Much to my chagrin, Bon fell in love with Diane, and the whole situation became uncomfortable.

When he realised he had no shot with her, Bon started turning up to my gigs totally wasted; he'd jump up on stage and sing very badly. It was so embarrassing my band had to try and persuade him not to show up anymore. One night in a suburban Melbourne gig, Bon was so wasted he could hardly stand up, but he stubbornly insisted that he wanted to get up and sing. Recently, someone told me they'd seen Bon fall right off the stage at one of my shows—this might have been the same night. It was all a bit sad. Bon was a truly nice human being, and one of our great lyricists and rock poets, with a fragile sensitivity that others didn't seem to notice.

Another remarkable thing about the Melbourne scene was the amount of work. We could fill the Station Hotel in Prahran on a Saturday afternoon, play a 10 p.m. gig that night, then play a third show at Bananas on the Esplanade at St Kilda at 2 a.m. The Station Hotel shows were legendary. Mark Barnes and Morag, who ran the pub, were—and I say this with all respect and affection—hardcore drinkers who seemed to attract fellow travellers like magnets. At these Saturday afternoon sessions, band and audience would drink themselves into a stupor, then all head back to Mark and Morag's house for an after-gig party.

NEED A VISIONARY

This would happen almost every weekend. If I was playing, the Dingoes, Ariel or other mates would get up and have a 'blow'—and vice versa. The drinking and partying was like a merry-go-round. But it did have to end eventually.

Festival Records, meanwhile, were asking me to record a third album. I'd patched up many of my differences with Richard Batchens, and was keen to get back into the studio. I was very excited about the songs I'd written in Melbourne. Like I said, I hear Melbourne 1976 throughout *Mainstreet Jive*; it still stirs up memories of that time for me. I also hear my American influences, people like Lonnie Mack, Little Feat, David Allen Coe, Danny O'Keefe, Randy Newman and some of the other great music we soaked up at the big house in Kew.

Back north, in 1976, Michael Hegerty and I based ourselves very close to the Bondi Lifesaver, Sydney's liveliest venue. Michael moved in with his sister and his girlfriend, while I found a pokey little place a couple of blocks away. I swear, the place was so small you couldn't even swing a cat without bashing it to death on all four walls. Michael and I became regulars at the Lifesaver, which was fast becoming known as the 'swap' (as in 'wife swap'), for reasons that will become clear.

I could never imagine another venue or a scene quite like the Lifesaver again. AC/DC ruled supreme, Dragon, Rose Tattoo, Mi-

Sex and the young infant bands, Midnight Oil and Cold Chisel—fresh out of Adelaide—were on the rise. Every night a truly great band would be playing at the Lifesaver. You could see Cold Chisel on a Tuesday night, Air Supply on Friday and on Saturday, AC/DC. Or perhaps Midnight Oil, Sherbet and Rose Tattoo. On the weekends the place was always packed way past legal limits.

Bondi was like a village, crawling with musicians. You couldn't walk a block without bumping into someone from a well-known band, a roadie or a rock journo. This created a fantastic camaraderie; I'd go out for coffee, or buy fish and chips down on Bondi Beach, then embark on a pub crawl that would last for ten or so hours, before ending up back at the Lifesaver just before midnight to catch the headliner. It was always scary playing the Lifesaver—not only was the room usually packed to the rafters, it was also full of my peers.

Inside the venue was an enormous fish tank that created a border halfway up the room, dividing it into the punters' section down in front of the stage, and the ultra cool VIP section up the back. The VIP section was raised a few feet so you could see the stage. It was always a shitfight getting in back there. On some nights it was less appealing, usually when it was patronised by some *Countdown* pop act, so Michael and I would hang out in the courtyard. We'd often bump into Phil Rudd, AC/DC's drummer, or one of the Chisel guys. We knew those supercilious little pop stars in the VIP area wouldn't be around for long.

NEED A VISIONARY

One night Phil Rudd and I got into a rave about Berlin.

'Those people are fucking weirdos, man,' Phil said.

He told me that AC/DC had just played their first gig at the Deutschlandhalle. Hundreds of fans were crammed down the front. Phil found out why these fans were called 'headbangers' when he began playing. Hundreds of them started bashing their skulls into the stage on every beat, every 'One-two-three-four' was accompanied by the crashing of flesh and bone on hardwood. After a few songs these guys were starting to bleed.

'When all this fucking blood was all over the stage, man, I just had to stop playing,' Phil told me. 'I couldn't take any more.'

Welcome to Berlin, Phil.

The downside of the Lifesaver was that heroin was considered dreadfully chic. I'd get so irritated trying to talk with friends who were scratching relentlessly or nodding off, both smackie traits. Worst of all, they all wore that smug, self-obsessed junkie's smile.

I knew Paul Hewson, Dragon's keyboard player and a great songwriter, but had no idea of his shocking medical state, which had something to do with a congenital condition in his spine. This led to his heroin addiction—it eased the terrible pain in his back. But I only learned this later. Paul used to really piss me off. I had enormous respect for him as a writer but would start getting agitated when he'd nod off into his beer while I was trying to talk to him about getting off smack and having more respect for his great talent. Sometimes I'd get scared that he'd overdose right there in front of me. That made me angrier still. I thought Dragon were fantastic; they should have become one of the biggest bands in the world.

So many strange things happened at the Lifesaver. I was once standing at the men's urinal and a fan of mine insisted on shaking my hand while we were standing there pissing away. One of the guys from a flavour-of-the-month band walked straight up and pissed all over our handshake. I would have smacked him in the mouth if I wasn't such a pacifist. I was still a bloody hippie.

I'd heard about people lacing the fish tank with illegal drugs and all the fish dying, which could well be true. The Lifesaver was that kind of place. The air was always blue with dope smoke and illicit drugs were everywhere. And yet no one ever seemed to get busted. As for me, I was getting into very heavy binge drinking; Southern Comfort or tequila were my poisons of choice. I'd only recently become a novice pot smoker, but Michael and I did like to drink ourselves stupid. Mandrax, a pharmaceutical that I guess was the forerunner to ecstasy, was rife at the Lifesaver; it encouraged all things sexual—and the Swap certainly was a hotbed of sexual activity.

Everybody was in bed with everybody, and if you were too drunk or stoned to make it to bed, well you'd just fuck in the car park or the dressing room or under one of the tables. The roadies used to notch up their visits to the 'Blue Clinic' in Macquarie Street—you weren't an elite roadie unless you'd tested positive for gonorrhea at least half a dozen times.

By comparison, my sexual career was somewhat conservative. I always had a steady girlfriend—they nearly all became de factos for a protracted period. My volatile Melbourne girlfriend landed on my doorstep one day and told me bluntly that she was moving in. This was not a woman to be messed with but I found her irresistible.

We soon slipped back into our alcoholic ways; heavy drinking became a way of life. Along with Michael and his girlfriend, I think we were all probably drunk every single day for months on end. It was not all bad though. My girlfriend was quite the connoisseur of fine food and wine, with fine cognac and even finer sex to follow. When she found a job as a waitress—and a new sense of purpose—our domestic life got a bit more under control.

In early 1976, when I began recording *Mainstreet Jive* with Richard Batchens at Festival studios, I insisted that I'd pick the band we used. The mood at the early sessions was hostile, very negative.

There was always an unpleasant power play going on between Michael Hegerty and Batchens, but there were some funny moments, too. At one point, when things were especially tense, Batchens relentlessly attacked Hegerty, criticising every little thing.

'Your bass is out of tune,' he told him.

We all sat out in the studio, waiting and waiting, as the drama unfolded. The glass window of the control room obscured Michael's hand; he was pretending to be turning the tuning peg on his bass, the source of the problem. From the other side of the glass, Batchens couldn't quite see what Michael was doing. Michael sat poker faced, pretending to fix the problem, but actually doing nothing.

'No, you're still flat,' Richard would call out. Michael would pretend to turn the tuning peg again.

'No,' Richard shouted, 'now you've gone too sharp!'

The rest of us sat out in the studio, straight-faced, trying hard not to explode into hysterical laughter. Michael probably should have been a comedian.

Batchens managed to sabotage my band and hired a line-up of his own. Fortunately, these players were among Australia's finest; most had played in the legendary jazz-fusion outfit Crossfire.

I'd learned from all the dramas that had plagued the 'Girls on the Avenue' recording a couple of years before. I decided to compromise and kowtowed to Richard more than I argued with him. I was passionate about this set of songs and didn't want to jeopardise the album. I kept my mouth shut most of the time. And I did get to meet guitarist Kirk Lorange and Rita Jean Bodine, a raunchy female singer from LA who was just starting to break into the American market. Although they lacked rock attitude the jazzy musicians produced a nice change from the distinct country feel of the previous album.

Festival, to their credit, adopted a much more respectful attitude to me. I think this is because the staff were much like the public service or corporate office workers. They had quaint archaic attitudes, and respected me for the fact that I'd survived a few years. I must admit that by toeing the company line a little more, rather than fighting for what I believed to be artistic integrity—and thereby pissing them off—the company did well by me. They came up with *Mainstream Jive* promotional ideas like coasters and matchbooks and T-shirts.

They allowed me to work with David Parker, a Melbourne photographer who went on to become a successful film producer. But there was one very odd incident. Michael Bradley, a childhood friend of mine, was also an excellent photographer. He submitted a great shot of a mime artist busking in Martin Plaza, which we used on the album's inner sleeve. Yet almost as soon as the record was released in late August 1976 we were threatened with an injunction by the mime artist who, having no rights in the picture, still managed to settle—out of court—with Festival for a tidy sum and immediately bailed for Paris, probably in search of Marcel Marceau.

Regrettably, *Mainstreet Jive* just didn't connect. I had moderate radio airplay but nowhere near enough to sell huge numbers. Critics praised the album, but the single, 'Suit

Yourself', wasn't a chart success. The album only made the Top Thirty.

It was time to re-evaluate my life. I'd started to view my art as a career, and realised that if I was to survive as a professional musician I was going to have to get used to compromise.

Not only did I have a new outlook, I had an excellent new band. Canadian expat Kirk Lorange joined on guitar, Michael played bass, Iain McLennan drummed and Tony Slavich played keyboards. Lori Balmer, who had sung back-up vocals on *Mainstreet*, also joined. Plus I had a new manager, Chris Murphy, who went on to big things with INXS.

Chris was reckless and probably brought me very near death on a few occasions, but he was one of the most passionate people I've ever known. His father was Mark Murphy, a Sydney entertainment agent from the 1960s, who died of a heart attack in his early thirties. Chris always seemed to be on a mission.

The first real fight I ever had with Chris was because I refused to appear in Tamworth after an in-flight drama. Kirk and I arrived at Sydney airport, ready to fly north, while Chris had driven the rest of the band up in a rental car. Kirk and I watched the crew prepare the Fokker Friendship for departure. My first feature story had just run in *Rolling Stone*, and I was trying to read it, while Kirk kept making paranoid comments about the safety of the plane.

I then realised that he'd smoked a big hash joint and was very stoned. He rambled on and on.

'That plane's just a big sardine can held together with flimsy rivets,' Kirk told me.

My irritation turned to annoyance as we took our seats up the front of the plane. I just wanted him to shut up. The plane took off and I assumed it was normal for a Fokker Friendship to struggle up to 20,000 feet. And the plane did seem to be struggling for some minutes. I had my head buried in *Rolling Stone*, but Kirk kept persisting with stories about the engines cutting out.

'Look at that!' he shouted at me, pointing outside the window.

Aw shit! The propeller was totally dead. This couldn't be normal. A hysterical hostie came out of the cockpit; an older hostess started threatening to slap her if she didn't calm down.

'We're gonna die!' she sobbed.

Oh shit.

Panic spread through the plane. Children were crying and their mothers were praying. Kirk, still very stoned, looked like he was going to beat all of us to death's door—the older hostie thought he was having a heart attack. Then the other engine stopped dead. The plane was gliding with no power. For the first time in my life I was knockin' on heaven's door.

Yet I felt quite calm. All of a sudden dying didn't seem so bad. I was caught in this daze with one eye on Kirk, thinking, well, this is it, huh?

A Tamworth grazier, resplendent in tweed jacket, handlebar moustache, farmer's hat and jodhpurs, came striding down the aisle and began bashing on the cockpit door. I got up to help the hostesses who were trying to restrain him. He was out of control.

'Get out here, you bastards!' he screamed. 'I demand to speak to the managing director of this airline. This little debacle will make me miss my meeting in Tamworth and I'm gonna lose a quarter of a million dollars. I'll sue you lot for this!'

I cracked up laughing.

'Can you believe this guy?' I asked Kirk, laughing hard.

'Mate,' I said to the frantic farmer, 'we're gonna die. What the hell are you talking about, you fruitcake!'

A few other people were beginning to see the absurdity of this farce. Then we looked out the window and saw Sydney airport. We'd been gliding for God knows how long; there was no sound, just the gentle whoosh swish of the jetstream. The pilot, who hadn't said one word during this drama, spoke over the intercom.

'Good afternoon, ladies and gentlemen, this is Captain Johnston and I've been your pilot aboard today's flight. You may have noticed we've experienced a slight mechanical problem and have decided to return to Sydney airport. There is absolutely no cause for concern and we will have another plane ready for immediate take-off.'

A slight mechanical problem! Was this guy for real?

A glider landing, as I found out, is so soft you can hardly sense when the aircraft has actually touched the tarmac. When we filed off the plane, Kirk suddenly became full of bravado, whereas I descended into shock.

I phoned Chris Murphy.

'There is no way,' I told him, 'that I'm getting onto another Fokker Friendship. No freakin' way.'

Chris was upset; in fact he screamed back that he wanted to kill me. His temper, as I was quickly learning, could be terrifying, but I would rather he killed me than I go down in a plane crash.

I think that was the first time I made the front page of the daily newspapers. I must admit that 'ROCK STAR IN PLANE CRASH' looked really cool. Hey, what's good for Buddy Holly and Otis Redding . . .

I did rejoin Chris and my band the next day—by jet, mind you—and so began my first real tour. Just days after the near thing with the plane, Chris was driving the car like a madman along a particularly treacherous stretch of mountain road. He was singing Neil Young's 'Cripple Creek Ferry' out of tune at the top of his voice while careering all over the slippery, winding road. He missed a corner and suddenly we were perched over a cliff with a drop straight down of a couple of hundred feet.

Michael Hegerty and I crawled out of the car.

'You fuckin' arseholes,' Chris screamed. 'You fuckin' get back in this car right now or I'll get out and smash yer fuckin' faces in. *I am ordering you to get back in this car!*'

By now Chris was sitting in the car all by himself, bashing the steering wheel while threatening to bash us, as the front of the rental gently rocked up and down in the strong mountain winds. Right then a farmer appeared around the corner in a Jeep complete with towbar and chains and hauled Chris and the car off the cliff. Another close call.

10

'Goodbye Tiger—
Chasing those dolce vita times'

Goodbye Tiger

One evening a girl who worked at Festival invited me to her place for dinner. I became a little intoxicated on white wine and she produced an application form for an Arts Council grant. We filled it in together while I was still a bit inebriated and I forgot all about it. Several months later, Festival GM Phil Matthews stopped me as I was going in through the front door of the building. He was waving a piece of paper.

'Congratulations!' he said.

'For what?'

Phil handed me two pieces of paper. One was an acknowledgement of receipt and the other a cheque—just enough for me to buy a round the world air ticket. I don't know what the hell I put in my application, but I'm sure it was pretty silly.

The bizarre thing about the Australia Council grant, as I soon found out, was that recipients aren't required to account for anything. I was finally asked for a report of the work I had produced in 1976—in 1996. Fortunately for the Australia

Council I wrote the set of songs for *Goodbye Tiger* with my grant so at least someone—me—produced something of worth.

I went straight down to Qantas and bought my ticket. I then phoned Volker Cornelius in Berlin and told him I'd be returning soon. However, I had committed to working on a surfing movie called *Highway One* with David Elphick and Steve Otton, which I had to complete before charging off overseas.

Elphick had a beautiful place at Palm Beach where I would regularly work with him. David preferred weekends so we could kick on a little bit. One Saturday my girlfriend and I went up to David's studios in the afternoon and ended up partying very hard all night. We stumbled out at about 6 or 7 a.m. and drove just around the bend and onto the Palm Beach Road.

Her car hadn't been all that well recently—despite the fact that it was an almost brand new Nissan Z—and as we approached Palm Beach the thing just died. There were quite a few happy suburban families meandering down to the beach and coming out of the milkbar with their Sunday papers as we started abusing each other. Loudly. One of us had to take the long walk down the road to phone the NRMA. My girlfriend drew the short straw and stormed off.

I grabbed a piece of paper and wrote these lines: 'The Sunday drivers are cruising round, wish they'd all go back to town.'

It was ironic, really—I lived in Bondi Junction but because of these lyrics and the song where they'd end up, 'Deep Water', some saw me as poet laureate of the Peninsula. I would have liked to have been poet laureate of anything, but I was just a Bondi boy.

My relationship was deteriorating rapidly; the more obsessive my girlfriend became the more I wanted to end things. There was an immediate pressure on me to deliver the *Highway One* album, and a strong single would enhance the film's chance of success. But my stormy domestic situation was really starting to hinder my work. Michael gave me a very strong joint one night, I got seriously stoned and 'Capricorn Dancer' flowed out of me like water. For some reason I had a mental block on a fourth stanza for the song, but Richard insisted that the song was fine just repeating lines from the second. It worked.

My personal life was by now resembling a Stephen King novel so Richard got me into Festival studios for five days and we recorded an impressive volume of material for the album, 'Capricorn Dancer' included. Then I was out of there. It was time to head back to Berlin.

I began leaking news about my secret departure to my best friends, including David N. Pepperell and Dave Dawson. Pepperell jumped on the first plane to Sydney, already drunk, and insisted that we were going to see the gonzo writer Hunter S. Thompson at the Town Hall. He had a few of his Melbourne bohemian buddies in tow—also inebriated—and I went along very reluctantly.

David and his crew began interjecting loudly. Thompson was handling it, but only just. Pepper must have had a lot of speed because he was garbling garrulously and not giving Thompson a chance to reply. I was embarrassed and physically dragged David and his mates out of the Town Hall and into a sleazy pub over the road. We proceeded to get totally obliterated. We then went back to David's hotel in Potts Point where he ordered French champagne by the case. We partied till dawn and trashed his room in the process.

I had been sneaking musical equipment over to Berlin without my girlfriend knowing. They were my only real possessions. The day after the Thompson debacle I had the worst dispute yet with my girlfriend (my blinding hangover didn't help), so I stormed out of the flat and grabbed the first taxi I could find.

'Mascot airport, thanks,' I told the driver. 'And fast, if you could.'

Somehow my girlfriend found out about my escape. I ran into the airport—I still had valid papers for Berlin—and asked to be put on the first flight to Germany. There was one leaving soon. Perfect. I went inside the gates, seeking sanctuary, and just as we were starting to board, I saw my girlfriend outside, stamping her feet furiously and shaking a fist at me. I could still see her from my window seat; by the time they towed the plane back I could see she was crying, her face pressed to the glass. I deeply regretted slipping away under cover of night, but this relationship could not possibly have succeeded. We were both alcoholics, which, as any educated person knows, is one evil drug. I really had to drag myself away from her, for both our sakes. But I may have shed a tear, too.

I arrived in Germany the next day in a blinding snowstorm, having drunk a lot on the plane to ease my fear of flying. Volker and Andrea had only recently moved into a new apartment on Kaiser Wilhelm Strasse—much smaller than Klausenerplatz, but better situated. There was plenty of room for me.

When we arrived back at the apartment, I sat down and wrote 'Goodbye Tiger' all in one go. Dr Pepper called me 'Tiger', an old ocker expression of endearment. It's a real blokey nickname. The lyrics may sound fictitious and poetic but the words are virtually literal, and journalistic in their own way. The lyric was pretty much a transcript of our conversation back in David's hotel room a few nights before, my itching to be 'chasing those dolce vita times'.

It was nearly the end of Volker's semester at the university, and he'd rented a farmhouse on Nørre Nebel, the northernmost tip of Denmark. It had been a long time since I'd last seen Denmark and I was keen to return. We drove up to Hamburg, and I met Andrea's mother for the first time. She was a senior editor at *Stern*, the famous German magazine, and was a fascinating person to talk to. At the end of the war she'd ended up with an anonymous American soldier when the troops arrived in Hamburg. One night later and he was gone, leaving her with Andrea.

From Hamburg we drove through incredible blizzards to Nørre Nebel; the farmhouse was just wonderful, like something out of an Ingmar Bergman film. (Maybe it was.) It snowed so hard we could barely get the front door open, so we agreed to stock up on supplies and not bother leaving. I holed up in my room with the door closed and songs flowed out of me. I couldn't have dreamt up a better environment for writing.

I already had the basic idea for 'Deep Water', an invented story about Michael Hegerty's sister, Christine, down on Bondi Beach. Christine was a real ham, hence all the stuff about doing the foxtrot on the beach at night with the fireflies dancing in the promenade lights. I decided to marry that part of the song to the Palm Beach Road incident. I'd been toying with the idea of writing an opus that would encapsulate Sydney life within that seven minutes and it all fell into place.

'Lucky Country' was next, another quick and painless birth. The first time I went out in the snow I walked down to the frozen beach; it all struck me as incredibly weird. There I was, up near the North Pole, writing songs about the Antipodes. And yet it was so easy. I'll die happy knowing that I wrote three of my best songs—'Tiger', 'Deep Water' and 'Lucky Country'—in just a few days. Bang, bang, bang!

We returned to the city and I settled into Berlin life as if I'd never left. I was back with my old friends and began speaking 'Berliner' immediately and effortlessly. I'd enjoyed my few years back in Oz, but I felt better in Berlin, more at home. There was something about my life there that was much more fulfilling, although I wasn't sure exactly why. I began making plans to put down roots in Germany.

Royalties from Australia kept me living quite well for a few months, while I hustled English and German record companies for a deal. I'd always found those running the German record companies to be very frustrating to deal with. However, I befriended a really cool guy in Hamburg, by far the best industry person I'd met in Germany. He'd worked for a big label but had decided to go it alone. I spent lots of time in Hamburg, staying with Andrea's mum and trying to formulate some sort of plan with the guy.

Unfortunately, his spirits were low and he wasn't sure if he even wanted to stay in the industry. But he had enormous belief in me. I told him that I felt that if handled correctly I could break out of Germany and into the United States. Sadly, we just couldn't get any of the German record companies to commit to the extent that we hoped.

I was also trying to consolidate my contacts in England, but was restricted by not having the money to make unlimited trips to London to hustle. I did get one call for a meeting in London, and was in the middle of a week-long fasting diet I'd spotted in *Stern*, surviving on nothing but water (after another week of scaling down). I went to London and did not let one morsel of food pass my lips, yet I think I've never felt better my entire life.

Nothing came of the meeting and I started to just drift along. I still wanted to stay in Europe, but back in Australia, 'Capricorn Dancer', which came out as a single in early 1977, looked like it was going to be a hit. Festival's Phil Matthews implored me to come home and promote 'Capricorn Dancer' and record one more album for the label. I made it very clear that Richard Batchens and other people at Festival wouldn't mess with my music ever again. I was really starting to assert my independence. Phil, an all-round great guy, kept sending me reassurances by telegram.

I'd hit a very big fork in the road. Was I an Australian or a universal traveller? I was getting very confused.

I was dating Inge, the girl from 'Prussian Blue', and we had been getting along pretty well. But one night I took her to Romy Haag's and things changed rapidly. Romy Haag was the most incredible transvestite in Europe, rumoured to be a partner of David Bowie. People came from all over the world to check out his club. It was necessary to book weeks in advance and I kept the evening as a special surprise for Inge.

We arrived and Inge was awestruck by what she believed to be a nightclub full of the most beautiful women in Europe. The floorshow was as close to Liza Minnelli's *Cabaret* as I was ever going to see. We'd been there for a while when one particularly camp act came on stage and Inge began to smell a rat. Or a bloke.

Just then, Romy Haag came swanning up to the bar and sat next to us. Inge was gazing at Romy's diamonds and beautiful mink hat and jacket. I'd had a few drinks and started teasing her. Romy was beautiful; we couldn't stop looking at him. Suddenly the penny dropped, and Inge burst into tears, ran out of the club, jumped into a taxi and fled. She refused to see me again.

That was the clincher. I called Phil Matthews.

'I'll come home,' I said, 'but I want to visit the Dingoes in San Francisco on the way back.'

He agreed. In 1977 I left Berlin with a heavy heart and headed for America, landing in New York. I'd never been to the States before and I was completely awestruck.

Georg and his wife Sabine had been living in Manhattan for several years and were happy to have me stay for a few months. Georgie hadn't been having the best of times in New York; Sabine was totally immersed in her anthropological studies and Georgie had been very lazy with his English. They were living on Hudson Street in the East Village, just off Bleeker, and I immediately became Georgie's personal interpreter.

We hung out in all the legendary bars and folk clubs in Greenwich Village. Georgie would order 'to-killa-yew' (tequila), which had bar staff in hysterics and immediately endeared us to everyone. I went out every night, hanging out at CBGB's, Max's Kansas City, the Bottom Line and the Bitter End, all great clubs. I saw everyone from John Cale and Lou Reed to David Allan Coe and the Nitty Gritty Dirt Band.

By day I shared some bizarre experiences with the loonies who were so much a part of New York life. One day in Washington Square, Georg and I were both filming with our home movie cameras. A black guy came over and started yelling at us for filming him.

'We're not,' we assured him.

'You're racist pigs!' he screamed back.

Because Georgie's English was so bad, he misunderstood and began filming the guy. He tried to grab our cameras and we had to run for our lives.

I went to Times Square alone to see the Woody Guthrie biopic *Bound for Glory* and caught the subway at about 10 p.m. It was 32 below, absolutely freezing. I noticed something strange: passengers seemed to be moving down the train every time it stopped. After several stations I found out why. A homeless man entered our carriage naked, bar the garbage bag he was wearing. The smell was nauseating; I didn't even dare guess what was inside the bags he was wearing. Then I found out. When I finally looked at him, I saw that the garbage bag 'turban' he had wrapped around his head was full of human excrement.

After months of living in an apartment with twenty locks on the door, having watched some guy on live eye TV shooting twenty-two of his workmates because he hated the Jewish foreman, it all started to get a bit much. I decided to catch a plane to California, hoping for better things.

Georgie was devastated; he was trapped in New York with no friends. They'd had an ugly and frightening experience with a babysitter—one night he and Sabine came home and the babysitter had kidnapped Saskia, my goddaughter. It was only sheer luck that the babysitter changed his mind and dropped Saskia back outside the apartment, before disappearing forever. (I subsequently named one of my daughters Saskia.) I really felt for Georgie, but I had to keep moving.

The Dingoes were flying high. They were recording an album with Garth Hudson from The Band, and were being looked after by the Rolling Stones' manager. I stayed with Chris Stockley for a couple of days, but the band was busy, so I decided to take a Greyhound down to Hollywood.

The trip down the West Coast takes several hours, and during the drive it struck me that if you travel by Greyhound in America, and hang out at the YMCA, it must be easy to write songs—there are just so many colourful characters at that level of American life. There were drug dealers and card sharks and con men and all sorts on that bus.

We reached the depot at about eleven that night, and I was scared shitless. I'd walked straight into one of the heaviest areas in America, downtown LA, with a guitar, a camera case and a suitcase. The streets were swarming with pimps and drug dealers and gangs; it was a real-life *Taxi Driver* (different city, that's all). I hurried into the first hotel I could find. The dude on the desk was Hispanic, gelled-back hair in a ponytail, earring, the works. He spoke just like Cheech Marin.

When I got upstairs I saw why the room was so cheap. The light didn't work properly; the black-and-white TV was busted. When the hotel's neon sign reflected on my window I saw three bullet holes. I didn't need forensics to tell me someone had fired those bullets into this room. I was petrified. I couldn't go back out on the street now, so I'd have to wait it out till morning.

I sneaked a look under the starched white sheet and sure enough the mattress was covered in bloodstains. Of course, it could have been menstrual blood, but I tend to take the Raymond Chandler view. Welcome to LA. Next morning I couldn't get out of there fast enough and checked into the Holiday Inn with all the other tourists.

I wasn't destitute but I was on a shoestring budget and had to choose my tourist adventures carefully. Being a songwriter makes this a lot easier; I found it much more romantic to be drinking Coke with a hotdog at the bus depot on Hollywood and Vine than touring some studio.

I met a black dude who lived in the Greyhound station. He kept all his possessions in a locker. He'd ride the buses all night because it was safer and cleaner than sleeping on the streets with the other bums. Having been a bum myself in Europe, I started to nurture romantic notions of putting my guitar in a locker and doing the same, at least until I was discovered and became a big star! On second thoughts, that was a bit too clichéd for me.

I went to lunch with industry great Jerry Moss, the 'M' in A&M Records, which he'd established with Herb Alpert and was home to acts like The Flying Burrito Brothers and Burt Bacharach. He kept buying me Scotch and Coke and I got very intoxicated.

'I have to go,' I apologised after one too many, 'I'm just too pissed.'

Now, Americans have an entirely different definition of 'pissed'—it's short for 'pissed off'.

'What's wrong?' Jerry asked me repeatedly. 'What's upset you, Richard?'

'Whaaaat?' I slurred. 'I'm 'aving a great time. I'm really enjoying myself, Jer, but I'm just too pissed!'

It just didn't make sense to him. How could this weird Aussie be having such a great time if he's so pissed off?

I eventually booked a flight home to record my album for Festival, after spending some time with Chris Stockley in San Francisco. Part of me wanted to stay in America but I'd made the commitment; studio time had been booked for me to start work on *Goodbye Tiger*.

11

'Sitting out on the Palm Beach Road,
I'm so drunk and the car won't go'

Deep Water

Back in Sydney once more, I moved into a little flat, bought myself a bicycle and spent a lot of time just cycling around Bondi and hanging out. I made it very clear to Festival Records that I intended to remain committed to the 'art' of this next project; I simply wasn't comfortable being marketed as some pop star. I was very conscious of Jackson Browne, Little Feat and Randy Newman, real artists. They were my touchstones.

This appeared to present no problem to the label. They very gently steered me back to Richard Batchens. Politely yet firmly I told Richard I'd been very reluctant to return to Australia.

'Let's try and make this record without any feuds, okay?'

He agreed—but it was to be a short-lived peace.

We were to record 'Deep Water' first up. I went into the studio with Michael Hegerty on bass, Kirk Lorange on guitar and a funny Greek drummer called Jimmy Penson (tragically, the first mortality in my career, killed by a drunken driver on Bulli Pass). He'd played in a very successful boogie band called Blackfeather; he was a damned good drummer and all round nice guy. Jimmy was like a hilarious parody of an archetypical Greek. He wasn't dumb, but he would ham it up just for everyone's amusement.

In between sessions, we were playing at the Station in Melbourne to a more than packed house. The gig was going really well but a grumpy Kirk Lorange kept screaming at Jimmy to 'lay back', musician talk for 'slow down the beat'. Jimmy had the dopiest look on his face as if he didn't understand. Every time Kirk would scream 'lay back', Jimmy would lean further and further back on his drum stool until he was on the verge of falling off the stage. Michael and I were laughing so hard we could hardly play. That's Jimmy playing drums on 'Deep Water' and 'Capricorn Dancer'.

Also in the studio with me were Cleis Pearce (on viola) and drummer Greg Sheehan, who'd both played in an 'acid jazz' outfit called Mackenzie Theory. It didn't seem likely, but they were a good fit. Diane also rejoined what was to become the notorious 'Goodbye Tiger' band.

Feuding erupted almost immediately between Batchens and the band. Kirk and Michael joined together in one of several factions; they regarded themselves as the 'sane' members of the band. Greg and Cleis were Balmain hippies who survived on macrobiotic food and LSD. Richard Batchens's main ally was John Frolich, the engineer, a Palm Beach hippie and original New Age guy. I was just the pivot for everyone else to cling on to.

The project lapsed into an orgy of booze and drugs. Half the band was tripping, the rest were stoned. I was still not much of a druggie, and as usual found the drug taking irritating, but tried to remain tolerant for the sake of the album. *My album.* Soon enough, though, I became a complete drunk, unable to cope with the relentless tension. I kept waiting for the next bomb to go off.

I was totally miserable. I desperately wanted to quit the album because I really didn't believe that we'd ever finish it—or survive. But I knew I'd relinquished the opportunity to relocate to America or to Europe, and was damned if I was going to let this bring me down.

How on earth we managed to record that album in that state still amazes me. Because I was short of material, I came up with an idea.

'Let's get totally trashed,' I announced, 'and I'll write a song "while-u-wait".'

Why not?

Kirk was stoned and late for the session. By now Batchens and I were drunk; we started calling Kirk a 'pussy' and a 'wimp'. After threatening to quit there and then, Kirk reluctantly plugged into the powerful amp that I'd hired for him, a 100-watt Marshall. I sat in an isolation booth utterly wasted, and just started playing. I was so drunk, I started doing a Captain Beefheart impersonation, growling rather than singing. You can hear me bursting into laughter throughout the track, which was called 'I Can Talk to You'.

The intensity was incredible. Kirk detested Cleis and vice versa; the dogfight between these two for solos I think created one of the best moments in Australian recording history.

As the album progressed, things worsened, if that was possible. Richard stayed drunk; I was either stressed or depressed. Batchens still insisted on humming 'hook' lines to Kirk Lorange, which caused enormous friction between them. Ironically, the 'guitar hooks' on 'Deep Water' and 'Lucky Country' were actually Richard Batchens's, so maybe his ideas weren't that bad.

Kirk and Richard's war climaxed during a night at the 'Pyrmont Hilton', where a scuffle broke out. Richard had to be restrained from wanting to seriously bash Kirk; he may have even landed a couple of punches. Kirk quit the album and I went to meet Jim White, the general manager of Festival.

'I can't work with Richard,' I told him.

I felt really awful, because I loved Richard in a very odd sort of way, but he was so out of control that he was sidelined. I set to work producing most of Kirk's guitar parts myself but Richard produced Kirk's solo on 'Deep Water', which he played while he was perched right up against the brand new $10,000 speakers in Festival's control room, his guitar literally five centimetres from the speaker cone. I shudder to think of the consequences had we blown up their new speakers. Sounds great, though.

Richard Batchens eventually talked his way back onto the project, and we closed off the studio from the outside world, including the band. We brought in session players to apply the finishing touches.

The last stages of the album were intensely emotional. Richard and I were still reeling from all the earlier dramas. I must say, in all fairness, that Richard did an excellent job with recording my vocals; no longer did he demand repeated takes. I would never concede that those vocals are my best, but this is where I really learnt to sing in a recording studio.

We ended the album as we'd begun: drunk. We'd drink in the afternoons and watch the sun go down over Pyrmont— and then we'd walk down to the studio and work until early morning.

I have always been frustrated about the lack of real insanity or 'pushing the envelope' in Australian recordings. My theory about the enduring popularity of *Goodbye Tiger* is that it was the first homegrown album that captured a journey to the outer stratosphere. All the anger and bitterness actually manifested itself into something quite passionate and beautiful. Don't ask me why; it just worked. It was worth the pain.

There was a lot going on elsewhere in my life during the few months of recording *Goodbye Tiger* (a marathon by local standards, incidentally). I was befriended by the legendary radio DJ Billy Pinnell, who introduced me to Stan 'the Man' Rofe, the music guru of 3XY. Billy so passionately believed in 'Capricorn Dancer' that together we gatecrashed the pub where Rofe drank in private.

Stan the Man *was* Melbourne radio; quite frankly, this little stunt could have seriously damaged both our careers. It was a very risky punt. But we managed to get Stan on side, and he singlehandedly made 'Capricorn Dancer' a big hit and set up the *Goodbye Tiger* album nicely. Even before the album appeared in October 1977, pre-orders had exceeded 35,000 copies, 'gold' status, a first for me.

I was still frequenting the Lifesaver and it's there I met the first of three Susies in my life (so far). She'd been married to a fairly successful rock guitarist but the marriage didn't last. Straight away, I was besotted with her—to me, Susie was a girl in a woman's body.

There were some good times, too. Michael Hegerty and I used to frequent the Astra on Bondi Beach, eat French or Mexican food in the many restaurants on Bondi Road, get pissed and invariably end up at the Lifesaver. The one time Michael and I took Mandrax was during some of the early photo shoots for the *Goodbye Tiger* cover.

Chris Murphy was still in charge; however, Michael Chugg, a business associate of Chris's, slipped in behind his back and asked me around to his place in McMahon's Point. It was the first of several thousand nights with Chuggie that I have great trouble remembering. Some are lost completely.

Chuggie was a human dynamo. It was as though this giant rollercoaster that had lain dormant for a long time had now roared into action. I was cruising through life quite nicely enough, but suddenly the rollercoaster took off with Chuggie at the helm—whoosh—and life started moving at a great pace.

Chuggie ordered us into serious rehearsal, barking at us like some sergeant major. He yelled at photographer Violet Hamilton—'Get the fuckin' cover finished!'—and at the record company—'Get the fuckin' thing in the shops!'

I had been *Rolling Stone*'s singer, songwriter and artist of the year in 1976—and was voted singer/songwriter and artist of the year for 1977. And I remained in great favour with JJJ, 2SM, 3XY and most radio stations around the country. Chuggie enhanced all this and, I must admit, was a damn good manager. With the record finally in the stores and the charts—where it would stay for six months—we hit the road, hard.

The band was a bizarre combination of personalities: Diane McLennan, Cleis Pearce, Greg Sheehan and mainstays Michael Hegerty and Kirk Lorange. We played the Sandgroper in Perth, the Marryatville in Adelaide, the Lifesaver, Bombay Rock in Melbourne and I reckon a thousand other gigs in between, every gig a full house. This really was the golden age of Australian rock'n'roll.

Perhaps what makes a lot of bands great is the internal warring that goes on night after night. The *Goodbye Tiger* line-up was a band of extremes, and nobody knew, including me, whether we'd be the greatest band in the world or the worst on any particular night.

Americans Fleetwood Mac were renowned for their volatile in-house dynamics, but they had nothing on us! Kirk was continually flirting with Diane, who'd been going through a tough break-up with her husband, parading around in his undies trying to lure her into his web. Kirk hated Cleis and Greg, who were total acid hippies with their own little love nest going on. Michael and I kept getting totally wasted, especially when Chuggie was around.

One fateful night in Adelaide, after we'd played one of our greatest gigs, Diane and I somehow became detached from the rest of the band and ended up in a night of furious and passionate lovemaking in a hotel somewhere on Hindley Street. Seriously, it was on par with something you'd see in an Italian 'art' movie, and almost as hilarious.

Thus began the most bittersweet relationship of my whole life with this remarkable woman. I always thought Diane knew she was headed for a short life—sadly, she was right—so she crammed in more living than others would in ten lifetimes.

When we woke up the next day, the consequences of our actions really hit home, so Diane started drinking to get drunk and stay drunk. She simply could not tell her husband that their marriage was over. We flew to Perth, drinking all the way, and my voice started giving out on me before we'd played one gig in the west. I came down with pharyngitis; I literally had no voice whatsoever.

The enforced lay-off cost me a fortune, but allowed everyone to laze around the motel swimming pool for several days. When my voice finally returned, we played our biggest West Australian gig, a huge hippie festival in a remote rainforest. The stage was set on the banks of a beautiful river, and as we played, there were naked hippies swinging Tarzan-style across the front of the stage, flying through the air into the river. The air was thick with marijuana and people were tripping off their heads on mushrooms and LSD. It was like going to hippie heaven.

There were many equally legendary gigs on that tour. We played up on the Noosa headland in the lifesaving clubhouse and blew out the power for half the district. Noosa was not the sophisticated resort it has become and it took hours for the power to be restored—when it did we kept playing into the morning. Ian 'Molly' Meldrum had a very wealthy friend up there, and Diane and I floated around his swimming pool, carefully ensuring that my cocktail didn't sink. I took a photo of Chuggie the next morning, which ended up on my *Past Hits and Previews* album. It's an everlasting testament to just how big a night it was.

12

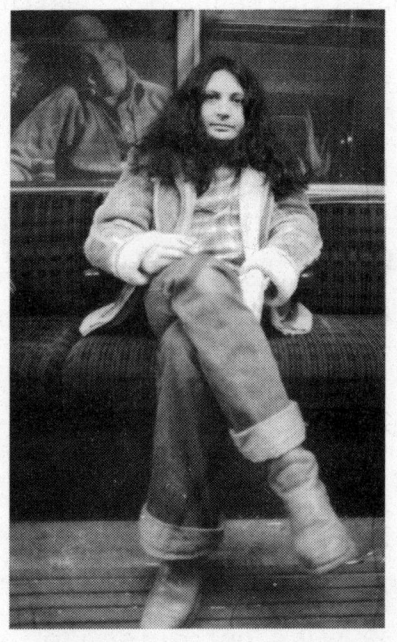

'i just got back from the South Row,
And i'm out on the edge again'

Out on the Edge Again

The only place in Australia we didn't tour during 1977 was the Northern Territory. We played hundreds of gigs. When there was nowhere left to play we would go back and play the same gigs again and again. Our tour manager Neil was an abrasive type, who had a habit of yelling every little piece of information. It didn't help the psychological and emotional stress that built on the tour; I felt as though we were endlessly driving up and down Highway One pursued by a huge twister. This chaos, however, was of our own design; the heavy drinking certainly didn't help.

I played one of the legendary Gold Coast clubs and the venue was packed, the crowd almost out of control. After the gig, Diane and I had a tiff. She was busy talking to some friends of hers and I was very drunk and wanted to get back to the motel and get some sleep. I managed to wrestle the car keys from her, and stumbled out into the car park and into the band car. I hadn't had a driver's licence for some years but managed a perfect three-point turn out of the car park and on to the road.

But I was so drunk I hadn't noticed that I'd nudged a telegraph pole. No matter how much I accelerated, the car was not moving an inch. There were clouds of blue smoke coming from the burning tyres. I was so clueless that I asked a passer-by why the car wasn't moving.

'Richard, mate,' he replied through the driver's window, 'it's not moving because you're wedged up against a telegraph pole.'

When the inevitable happened and the police arrived, over 200 of my loyal fans, who were hanging around the car park, whipped up some bizarre story about a gang of bikies running the band car off the road. Diane had appeared by this time.

'I'm the driver,' she lied to the cops. Because she hadn't had much to drink, we got away with it. (I'm not proud of this, by the way, and now wouldn't drive under the influence. It's hard enough sober.)

We also played the Stagedoor Tavern, a notorious Sydney venue near Central Station. I'd been to dinner with Chuggie and was quite inebriated by the time we arrived backstage. Like most venues, it was packed way beyond its legal limit; the accumulated sweat was condensing and raining down on all of us. It was like some crazy rock'n'roll sauna.

The band and crowd were really connecting and I figured it was time to do something spectacular. I spied what I thought were metal railings attached to the ceiling. I climbed on top of the PA stack, dived off the huge speakers and caught the railings. The crowd erupted and I started swinging jungle-style.

But then my weight wrenched one of the railings out of the ceiling. They turned out to be water pipes. Suddenly, torrents of water flowed from every which way; it was pandemonium. God knows what might have happened if the power had shorted out—electricity and water can make a fairly lively combination.

Like something straight out of the film *Almost Famous*, a sixteen-year-old schoolboy named Ed St John had been commissioned to write a feature story on me for *Rolling Stone*. After that gig, Ed accompanied Neil and me back to a hotel in Kings Cross at about 1 a.m. Neil and I were both smashed; when Ed asked Neil if he would mind taking a walk through Kings Cross to find some batteries for his recorder, we turned on him like jackals. As Ed later told me, he asked me one question and my answer dragged on for over two hours. I worried about this for some weeks until Ed's absolutely glowing story on me and *Goodbye Tiger* hit the newsstands.

The crazier the band became, the more our legend spread, especially within the hippie/surfing subculture. I was obsessed with taking the show to a higher level every night; I became more and more decadent. I was terrorising journalists and record company people, and picking fights with people I perceived to be bourgeois and reactionary. The irony was clear—the more of an *enfant terrible* I became the more people paid to see me and my travelling madhouse.

But this wasn't an act. I simply wasn't coping with all the attention. I was getting drunk to stay drunk, and when the pressure became too much I would turn into a raging bull and devastate hotel rooms. I had genuinely turned psycho. It got to the stage where I just couldn't cope; I had to get off the road.

I stayed up all night drinking myself into a stupor in Launceston and the next morning refused to board a flight back to the mainland. Neil the tour manager physically dragged me all the way out to the tarmac, but they'd just closed the doors to the plane. He went nuts and stood in front of the 737, screaming and waving his arms like a mad man.

'Open the fucking doors!' he yelled at the astonished pilot.

Amazingly, the pilot reopened the aircraft door and Neil dragged me up the steps like a drunken sack of spuds.

My record was on the charts, my songs all over the radio, my concerts were sold out—and I was an absolute mess.

In Melbourne, Festival provided a presidential suite in a five-star hotel for me to do interviews. All my rogue mates turned up and drank the mini bar dry, not just once, but eight times in one day. Late that night, Michael Hegerty wrenched two fire extinguishers from the walls and ran screaming down the hallway spraying foam everywhere. I was incensed and forced Michael to mop up the damage with towels until dawn.

The next night we played the Tiger Lounge in Richmond to a full and drunken audience. *Goodbye Tiger* was number one in Melbourne that week, but when I proudly introduced the song, I was pelted with beer cans. I was shocked. Someone in the band got in my ear and told me that the Richmond football club—otherwise known as the Tigers—had just lost the grand final. Having some New South Welshman singing 'goodbye tiger' was simply too much!

But it wasn't all lunacy in my life. A couple of years earlier, I'd been befriended by George Wayne. George started out in commercial radio in Australia but had relocated to Los Angeles for eight years, where he became very popular with many of the musical icons of the seventies, especially Little Feat and Jackson Browne. When George returned to Sydney, he curiously opted to work at 2JJ rather than a corporate network, but maintained close links with his famous friends in LA.

George had been sending copies of all my albums to Jackson Browne. Jackson particularly liked *Goodbye Tiger* and George set up a phone conversation. As time went on, Jackson became more interested in me as an artist and talked me up to his record company, Elektra/Asylum, owned by music mogul David Geffen, who also managed Jackson. Jackson was seriously considering becoming my producer and developing my career in partnership with Geffen.

George Wayne was also a close friend of Little Feat and when the band toured Australia in 1978, he arranged for Lowell George, the bandleader, to come in to the ABC so I could interview him live to air. I was a huge fan, but, sadly, Lowell was a 'no-show'.

Then we heard the gossip. Lowell's relationship with Little Feat drummer Richie Hayward had hit rock bottom. On this particularly bad day, Lowell had locked himself in his hotel room, drunk a full bottle of Courvoisier cognac and snorted line after line of coke. I was in the wings at the Hordern Pavilion for the show that night, and was gobsmacked at how out of it Lowell was. Then an on-stage feud erupted between George and Hayward, they were cursing each other quite violently—and vocally. George played a guitar solo that was way beyond human comprehension, his intention being to end by hitting a note higher than any man had hit before. I was left reeling from the experience. Again, great art came through anger.

Around this time, Chuggie had fielded strong interest from Island Records in the UK; a very strong vibe was developing overseas. Chrysalis Records, United Artists, Arista and a number of other labels also expressed interest in me.

Festival was getting antsy, because my contract was up for renewal. It had taken them this long to get a substantial album from me, and Chuggie was out to get me the best possible deal. Thus began my first serious negotiation with a record company.

Alan Hely, the chairman of Festival, was well into his sixties, and was on medication. During one particularly lively Chuggie tantrum in the Festival boardroom, Hely simply nodded off. Chuggie and I were shouting, pacing around the table, and Hely was snoring. Scenes like this convinced me that Australian record companies just didn't take this game seriously.

Another time I was walking through the office from the Festival studio and heard the strains of Hawkwind, the radical English hippie-acid band, blasting at full volume from the boardroom. I looked inside and there was Hely, snoozing away again.

Hely just didn't seem to have any enthusiasm for my music or me; the negotiations with him and the label were tedious, drawn out. This problem, in my opinion, stalled my career offshore; I genuinely felt I could have become internationally successful.

In the end, Chuggie squeezed an impractically modest deal out of Festival, with disgracefully low royalties and a budget of $A36,000 to record overseas. The average American recording budget was closer to $A250,000, so we weren't looking too good.

However, Chuggie was not one to give up easily, and flew to England to talk to Phil Cooper, the general manager of Island Records. Phil was very excited about *Goodbye Tiger*. In a matter of days, the impetuous Chugg had Diane and me on a plane for Berlin. He ordered us to sit at Volker's place until Cooper called me to fly to London and sign the deal.

Diane and I arrived in Europe, anticipating a short stay. Unfortunately, thanks to Festival's inept handling of the Island deal, we were kept waiting for an inordinately long time. We decided to rent a little VW Golf and trek around Europe while we were waiting for Chuggie, Festival and Island to get it together. We drove through Germany, France and Holland and finally to Switzerland, before returning to Berlin.

Chuggie, meanwhile, had touring commitments in Australia, so left me to finalise the Island deal. Time began to drag and I was becoming concerned that something was going wrong, that I was being kept in the dark. Phil Cooper was becoming more and more unreliable at returning my phone calls. I could tell that something wasn't quite right.

However, the call finally came and Phil asked me to catch the first possible flight to London, and head straight to the Island office. At Heathrow, I was treated very badly by H.M. Customs. It turned out that a bunch of Aussie surfers had been busted that morning with smack, so it was hardly a great day to be an Australian traveller. They also noticed that I'd had the altercation with the police all those years ago. There I was, standing in the customs office, my hair down to my bum, pleading with them to let me go because I stood to lose a significant record deal if they detained me any longer. I finally convinced them of my story. But a lot of time had passed.

The taxi pulled up outside the Island building at about 5 p.m. and Phil came running out to greet me. He seemed very excited.

'Chris [Blackwell, Island's founder] will be here at six o'clock and we'll sign the deal then,' he told me. He invited me down to the corner pub for a pint and a sandwich, then we went back and played pool in the office rec room for a couple of hours. I met all the staff and was very elated, having the time of my life. Finally, a real record deal.

Blackwell phoned Phil a couple of times during the afternoon and everything appeared to be fine. At dusk, Blackwell phoned Phil to say that he would arrive in a few minutes. It was time. We stood outside as Blackwell drove up in his Aston Martin. He parked on the opposite side of the street, beckoning Phil—only Phil—to cross the street. They had a brief but angry exchange, then Blackwell jumped back into his car and drove off. I looked on, stunned.

'What the fuck was that all about?' I asked indignantly.

'Not now, Richard,' snorted Phil, just as indignantly.

'What do you mean, "not now"?' I insisted. 'What the fuck is going on?'

He told me to wait in the rec room until he was free and then we'd go down the pub. Once there, I started rapidly knocking back pints of bitter. I harassed the hell out of Phil and finally, when he was drunk, he spilled.

'Island can only pay a modest advance,' Phil said, something that was fine by Chuggie and me. 'But the problem is Festival,' he revealed. Festival, it turned out, were demanding an advance far outweighing my status. Phil also told me that Festival had been demanding a royalty that even exceeded that paid to superstar Steve Winwood. This was madness.

'Chris thought that Festival were just a bunch of Aussie colonials trying to bluff us,' Phil told me. 'He thought they'd back down eventually, there'd be a handshake and all would be fine.' But clearly that wasn't the case. Much to Chris Blackwell's shock, Festival became increasingly arrogant, and in the process derailed my record deal. It was over.

I was shattered. We returned to Berlin and all went out and got roaring drunk. That night, Diane and I swore that we would never return to Australia, it was just too soul destroying. I spoke to Chuggie, who told me that Chrysalis had also backed out, citing virtually the same reason.

But Chuggie had better news. He had a new partner in Los Angeles, a tough little dude called Merv Goldstein. There were some developments on the Elektra front; they wanted me in LA, now, to demo some new songs. Elton John's guitarist and Stevie Wonder's bassist were in the studio, waiting for me. The label loved *Goodbye Tiger*; if my new songs were equally good, a deal was on the cards.

'Richard, we're going to move to LA and live happily ever after.'

Once again, Chuggie ordered Diane and me onto a plane, heading west to America. I bade a sad goodbye to Volker and Berlin.

My fear of flying hadn't abated, so I headed straight for the airport bar. The barman, as luck would have it, was a German who had lived in Australia for a few years. As we talked, I knocked back several vodkas. Next thing I knew, a Lufthansa hostess was shaking me, urging me to fasten my seat belt. We were descending into LAX.

13

'Here on the razor's edge, stranded
here from my friends'

Hearts on the Nightline

Merv and Chuggie met us at the airport and swept us off to some swank Beverly Hills hotel. The next day we shifted base to a motel out in the San Fernando Valley. That night, for hours on end, some guy kept walking around the motel swimming pool, yelling gibberish. Around 11 p.m. he suddenly produced a handgun and started shooting up the place. Diane and I hid under the bed, terrified.

No one complained, no police showed up, and his shooting spree continued until well after midnight. It wasn't much of an introduction to Los Angeles.

'What's next?' I asked Diane, as we peeked out from under the bed.

The next day we checked into the Valley Hilton. The only problem there was the desk clerk, who wondered why I kept asking for Nadine.

'Who's Nadine?'

I was, in fact, asking for the key to room 318. Bloody accent.

I had a reasonable batch of songs that I'd written in Australia and Europe. Elektra's demo studio in the Valley was actually the old ranch of Monkee Mike Nesmith. We were booked for a 10 a.m. start. It was a big day. Huge.

Chuggie didn't have the hang of the LA freeway system; one wrong turn had us almost an hour late. Richie Zito, a fast-talking and very intense Italian New Yorker, was in charge of the session—and he was really shitty. Chuggie left me to face Zito, who abused the hell out of me for about 10 minutes.

'You'd better be the boy wonder the label says you are!' he muttered.

Reggie McBride, a big, round African American bass player from Stevie Wonder's band, joined the conversation.

'Chill out, Richie! Give the kid a break, man!' Then he turned to me. 'Hey, Rich, welcome to LA. Everybody's sayin' nice things about ya. I'm really looking forward to tracking some of your songs, man!'

'Thank Christ,' I thought to myself.

Richie Zito was still shitty, impatient to get started. I was sweating and shaking and more nervous than I'd ever been. I chose 'Stepping Across the Line', which ended up on my first greatest hits collection, and started to play the song for the band.

Zito interrupted me.

'Okay,' he snapped. 'Let's get started.'

I nervously insisted that there were a lot of chord changes in the song; perhaps I should play the whole thing.

No go.

'Fuck that! Roll tape!' Zito shouted.

The drummer counted in and we recorded about six songs in very quick succession, barely taking a break. But as soon as Richie heard some stuff back, his mood changed. By the end of the day we were good mates. I spent the next few days fixing and mixing my demos, and brought in back-up singer Rita Jean Bodine (who had sung on 'Suit Yourself' back in Sydney). Satisfied, I sent a cassette off to Elektra's A&R department.

We agreed to bring Michael Hegerty over to live and work with us in early 1979, and Merv moved us into a sprawling *Leave It to Beaver*-type house in Van Nuys, in the Valley.

It was time to finally try and get some order in my life. I decided to give up the booze for a while and cut back smoking. I was deadly serious about my American odyssey—I think it was the first time I'd ever really considered my health. It was actually great to stay sober and observe the circus that was going on around Diane and me.

Chuggie hosted frequent parties in a big house he shared in Agoura with the New Zealand-born guitarist Kevin Borich. The biggest bash was a lavish affair, with guests who included Owen Sloane, the leading entertainment lawyer in Los Angeles, Olivia Newton-John, Peter Rix, Billy Thorpe and a host of celebrated guests who constituted the so-called 'Gumleaf Mafia', the many Aussies based in LA.

Kevin Borich got pretty sloshed, and burst into an impromptu stand-up routine at Chuggie's expense. Kevin could have been a great comic if he wasn't totally besotted with the blues. Chuggie was boasting about our gang having transformed themselves from party animals into responsible health nuts.

'I'm even swimming twenty laps every morning,' added Chuggie, pointing in the direction of their pool.

KB interjected, letting everyone know that what Chuggie really meant was that he was turning himself around in the spa pool twenty times. Kevin also delighted in telling everybody how Chuggie and his roadie, Gerry Georgettis, would go jogging covered in garbage bags, convinced that they'd sweat off all the excess flab.

Kevin's tour-de-force, however, was the much-whispered 'race-calling' story. Chuggie, Kevin told the gathering, was an apprentice race caller from Burnie in Tasmania, who at the age of sixteen was recruited to call a national horse race from Adelaide. He arrived at a swank hotel and was told which horse was going to win—the race was fixed. Chuggie begged, borrowed and stole $2000 and put the lot on this horse, which we'll call 'BlahBlah'.

Chuggie was beside himself and extremely nervous; not only was this his big break as a caller, but he also had someone else's $2000 riding on this horse.

Chuggie began his call: 'They're out of the gates, DooDah's in front, DooDah's a nose in front, BlahBlah's coming up on the outside, BlahBlah's a nose in front. BlahBlah's half a length in front. BlahBlah's a length in front. BlahBlah's a length and a half in front—FUCK! THE CUNT FELL OVER!'

Chuggie dragged KB out of the room before he totally trashed his reputation.

❖

I met a Californian music publisher, Peter Burke, who'd just had some big hits and was flavour of the month in Hollywood. Peter was a handy ally—he was a good friend of Carol, the A&R exec at Elektra, who was not only the go-to person for my demos, but had also worked with The Byrds, musical heroes of mine.

A couple of weeks later, Carol finally called me at home and asked if I could spare an afternoon to come in and throw some ideas around. It was one of the greatest afternoons of my life—being treated like a star by a big US label, the home of Joni Mitchell, Jackson Browne and Warren Zevon, even Bob Dylan for a time.

'You,' Carol told me as we got comfortable, 'are the most exciting songwriter to emerge since Jackson Browne.'

As I tried to stay cool, she told me that it was her intention to use me as the main competitor in their battle against CBS and Bruce Springsteen. She spoke of a million-dollar promotional campaign, and—more importantly to me—putting me in the studio with Russ Titelman, who'd worked with Paul Simon and

James Taylor, or maybe Charlie (Chuck) Plotkin, her old boss, who'd worked with Springsteen and Harry Chapin. These were names I'd only dreamt about in Australia.

I hung out a little with Carol, a strawberry blonde who drove a fire-red Thunderbird convertible—real LA style. Then things seemed to drag; I sensed that the vibe was fading.

I called Peter Burke and asked him to investigate. What he came back with shattered all my dreams. It transpired that Carol had been caught up in a corporate power struggle against a weird misogynist named George. It was persecution, pure and simple.

But Carol was determined not to let me down; we'd just begun a wonderful friendship that had the potential to change our lives forever. She left Elektra and landed a job working for Chuck Plotkin in Nashville. But she planned one last meeting at which she'd play my demos and leave me with a deal at Elektra/Asylum.

She took the cassette into her antagonist's office and a normal A&R meeting degenerated into a psychodrama that ended with her enemy grabbing my cassette, ripping all the tape from its casing and smashing the case to pieces on the office floor. Carol ran from the building, sobbing. Rumour has it that a few months later George was committed to a mental institution.

I was totally devastated. Another big chance blown because of record label politics.

I turned to Chuggie for help.

'Get Alan Hely to sort out this mess, will ya?' I asked him in desperation.

Hely had recently boasted that he was a close chum of Joe Smith, the president of Elektra/Asylum. But Hely spent days avoiding us and Chuggie finally ran out of steam. My Elektra dream faded into thin air.

My royalties from *Goodbye Tiger* were starting to run dry. Chuggie, despite his best efforts, just didn't have the clout Stateside to get past first base, and he had other bands, other commitments, back in Australia.

In the late 1970s there were 15,000 professional lead guitarists in Los Angeles alone; the city was top-heavy with its own acts, let alone some long-haired dude from a little country seventeen flying hours away. But I was determined to stick around and see if I could make any headway.

Peter Burke, the American publisher, was also at the receiving end of some shabby treatment from Festival. Peter tried his darnedest to open some doors for me. He placed about six of my songs with various top line American artists, like the Pure Prairie League and Juice Newton. Newton was one of the top female artists in the world, and she actually recorded 'Capricorn Dancer' for a forthcoming album. But despite Peter's efforts to get Festival to negotiate a deal, they refused to respond. Peter eventually gave up on Festival and another big opportunity slipped away.

Top Albert Memorial, Kensington Gardens, London, 1968. AUTHOR'S COLLECTION

Above Royal Albert Hall, London, 1968. AUTHOR'S COLLECTION

Top My band in London, 1968. From left: Steve, Barry and Graham. AUTHOR'S COLLECTION

Above The Richard Clapton Band in the 1970s (from left): Gunther Gorman, Iain McLennan, Michael Hegerty, me and Tony Slavich. DAVID PARKER

Above Performing with the band in Parramatta in 1978. BOB KING

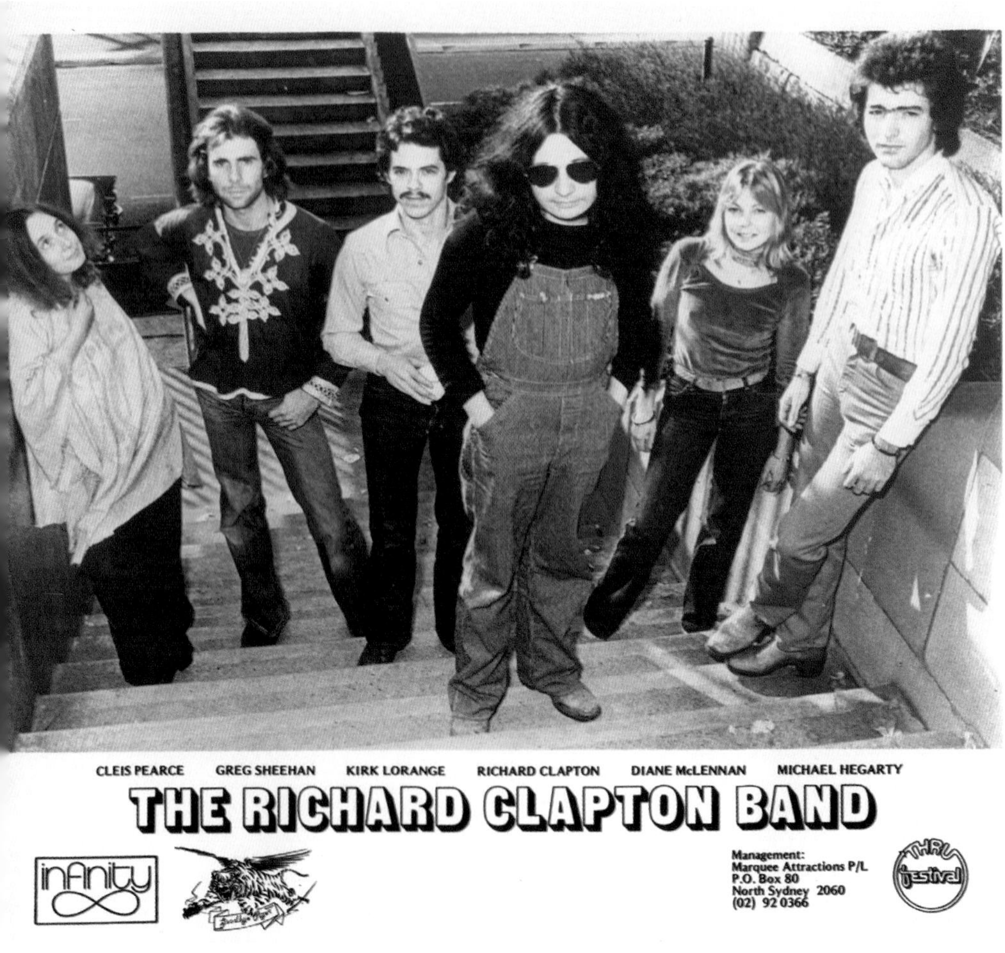

CLEIS PEARCE GREG SHEEHAN KIRK LORANGE RICHARD CLAPTON DIANE McLENNAN MICHAEL HEGARTY

THE RICHARD CLAPTON BAND

Management:
Marquee Attractions P/L
P.O. Box 80
North Sydney 2060
(02) 92 0366

Above The Richard Clapton Band in 1978, at the time the *Goodbye Tiger* album was released.
AUTHOR'S COLLECTION

Left An ad for a 1980 tour.

Above *The Girls on the Avenue* album cover shoot, 1975. GRAEME WEBBER

Top In a London cemetery, in the 1970s. AUTHOR'S COLLECTION

Above The apartment in Kantstrasse, Berlin, c. 1983. AUTHOR'S COLLECTION

Above The village church near the Nørre Nebel farmhouse, rented by Volker, where I wrote 'Deep Water' and 'Lucky Country', 1976. AUTHOR'S COLLECTION

Above The Richard Clapton Band, in the early 1980s (from left): Graham Thompson, Mark Myer, Mary Bradfield, me, Cos Russo and Harvey James.
TIM BAUER

Opposite (top, from left) Kirk Lorange, me and Richard Batchens during a recording session, 1977. AUTHOR'S COLLECTION

Opposite (bottom) Mark Opitz and me in Paradise Studios, 1980.
PHILIP MORTLOCK

Above The cover shot for *The Great Escape* album, which was released in 1982. PHILIP MORTLOCK

Left An image from *The Great Escape* cover shoot, on the deck of the *Oriana*. PHILIP MORTLOCK

Below A concept rough for *The Great Escape* album cover. PHILIP MORTLOCK

Above A promo shot for the *Glory Road* album. TIM BAUER

Opposite (top and middle) In Nice and Paris, 1987. AUTHOR'S COLLECTION

Opposite (bottom) Andrea, her daughter Charis and me, Berlin, 1987. AUTHOR'S COLLECTION

Top The cover shot from the *The Best Years of Our Lives* album. WENDY MCDOUGALL

Above The cover shot from the *Harlequin Nights* album. WENDY MCDOUGALL

Opposite With Jon Farriss, of INXS. PHILIP MORTLOCK

Top Susie and I with our baby daughters, Montana (left) and Saskia, 1990.
WENDY MCDOUGALL

Above At Wahroonga, in 2004. BRENDAN READ

14

'Sometimes when i feel you're sure
to change
i realise you're just playing to win'

Ace of Hearts

Back in Van Nuys, Michael Hegerty had arrived, along with Rick, our drummer from Melbourne. We didn't have green cards, so, with Diane, the four of us just sat around LA doing very little, and living off my royalties. When they dried up, Chuggie 'found' survival money. (Merv Goldstein insists that it was *his* money. Maybe so.)

I brought the band over because the plan was to find the best possible American producer and my guys would form the core players for the album. It didn't turn out that way, sadly. Michael and Rick managed to find work off the books and Michael ultimately forged a reasonable career for himself in America. I sat in the garage and tried to write songs.

Merv sent me for meetings with an interesting variety of record producers. I met with big timers who'd worked with Fleetwood Mac and the Eagles, as well as fledgling producers like Don Preston, a Southern guitar player who had been a long time hero of mine. He had worked with Leon Russell and was the guitarist on Joe Cocker's legendary 'Mad Dogs and

Englishmen' tour. But most of the people I encountered had an alarming propensity for cocaine and bourbon and 'life in the fast lane'. That Eagles song perfectly summed up LA in the late 1970s.

I stuck with my health kick, yet everywhere I went in LA there was a certain ceremony one had to go through. Instead of being invited to have a beer, your host would offer up a line of coke.

Diane and I went for a meeting with a certain LA producer. We met in his studio on a beautiful Los Angeles afternoon. The producer offered Diane and me a line of LA's finest. Initially I declined; I was still very wary of this stuff. But I caved in and after two or three lines I was telling the big time LA producer my life story. I couldn't stop babbling.

I finally ended up meeting Dallas Smith and decided that he was the right man for the job.

Dallas had worked on all the big hit singles for the blues band Canned Heat, along with an impressive résumé of prestige acts. He 'got' musicians; all the top players in LA loved him. Dallas introduced me to some of his mates—Bill Cuomo, who had co-written the number one 'Bette Davis Eyes' and was the top keyboard player in America; Ralph Humphrey, drummer for jazz great Chick Corea; Jerry Weems, Edgar Winter's guitarist; along with Dennis Belfield, who'd played bass with soul diva Chaka Khan's band Rufus. Gary Mallaber, currently Van Morrison's drummer, who'd played on Steve Miller's hits, also joined up. All big names, all great players.

I was happy to work with this bunch of Americans and see how my music would develop. Given that I had a lousy budget of 36 grand, most played for pocket money. Because I was a bit over-awed, I let go of the reins and the project took off on a course of its own. Despite this, *Hearts on the Nightline* was one of the happiest recording sessions of my career.

These guys were true musos, the real deal. For them, it wasn't about the money—luckily for me. They realised that anything could happen with the recording; it might be a hit, it might be a flop, but they were in for the ride. These players instilled the best values in me.

On Michael Hegerty's advice, I imported an Aussie keyboard player called Bruce Haymes. Eccentric didn't do Bruce justice. The day he arrived in Los Angeles, we were all busy in the studio and couldn't catch up with him until later. Bruce opted to do the tourist thing and took himself off on a bus trip to see the sights. From his seat at the back of the bus, he began to notice that white people seemed to be disembarking and more and more black people were boarding. He wasn't sure if he was imagining it, but ripples of laughter seemed to be directed at him by the other passengers.

Finally, a black dude down the front yelled out: 'Hey, ya honky motherfucker! Ain't you on the wrong bus?'

'Who me?' Bruce replied in astonishment.

The black passengers broke into hysterical laughter. Why wouldn't they? The bus had just rolled into Watts, the infamous black ghetto and sometime racial battleground. Bruce finally found his way back to the relative safety of the city.

Back at the studio, someone gave me a joint of Mexican weed.

'Be careful,' I was warned. 'It's absolute *feeelth*.'

I waited till late that evening, when the band had gone, lit up and settled in to watch the late movie. The dope was so strong I was almost hallucinating; I was glad to be in the security of my living room. Then a strange light, like an alien spaceship, enveloped the block where I lived. I heard the sound of a helicopter getting closer. Suddenly, two uniformed cops kicked in my front door and held pistols to my head. I almost had a cardiac arrest.

'You fuckin' motherfucker, get down on the floor!' they screamed at me. 'Get down on the floor, you fuckin' fuck!'

There was pandemonium; it felt like the helicopter was 2 metres above the house. There was a lot more screaming and swearing, before sanity prevailed.

'Oh, sorry,' the two dumb cops said to me, as they ran through the kitchen, across the backyard and over the back fence. Turns out I wasn't the armed burglar they were chasing; just some seriously stoned muso watching TV.

Chuggie's housemate Kevin Borich, meanwhile, was finishing a night of recording at Cherokee Studios in LA. Everyone was wired; they had to wind things up that night. Kevin had an American keyboard player, Rick, rushing through final keyboard parts and mixing the record on the run. Rick was out in the studio when a strange portly man, unshaved and looking like hell, walked through the front doors of the building and out into the studio. Rick immediately recognised Beach Boy legend Brian Wilson, and greeted him accordingly. He was royalty.

Wilson stood out there in the studio with glazed eyes staring straight at Rick. He muttered: 'Do you wanna do it?'

'Sorry, Brian—do what?' Rick replied.

'Do you wanna poo?' asked Wilson.

This turned out to be some illogical 'poo' game, but hell, it was Brian Wilson.

'Okay,' said Rick.

'POO!' Wilson yelled back. 'Now you do it.'

Rick and Brian played this weird game while Kevin's band rolled around the control room in hysterical laughter. After about 20 minutes, Wilson turned and calmly walked out of the studio.

Only in LA.

As you would imagine, living in Los Angeles for any extended period takes on an air of fantasy. Even a 3 a.m. trip to the supermarket is like a ride at Disneyland; there's plenty of fascinating characters to be found 24/7.

ACE OF HEARTS

We got quite a gang happening during our American sojourn. Ian Smith, who managed Australian Crawl and had tour managed me in Australia, was there, along with Noddy O'Donnell, my lighting roadie. We'd head off to Disneyland and jump on the thrillseeker rides; the Space Mountain, an indoor rollercoaster, was a particular fave. We used to love having 'greenhorn' visitors over from Australia and introducing them to these wild rides. Then we'd introduce them to the grub in the bottom of a tequila bottle. My specialty was a Pina Colada, which the Aussies would swill, unaware that the local Bacardi rum was 180 per cent proof.

Photography had become a real passion for me and I began experimenting with infrared nighttime photography. Diane and I would drive up to Zuma Beach or Laurel Canyon, and diligently set up a tripod and take weird photos with extreme exposures. We took a shot of me looking out over the San Fernando Valley from the Hollywood Hills. In the pitch black of night the lights of Los Angeles shone right through me; it was a fantastic, surreal concept.

When the shot was developed I contacted Graeme Webber in Melbourne to come over and take the shot professionally. Graeme had never been to the States before and we spent a few fun days running around LA. We did the whole Kerouac thing, getting stoned and driving around the city looking for B-grade movie scenarios and eating grubs out of tequila bottles. A very exhausted photographer came away with the photo that can be seen on the cover of *Hearts on the Nightline*, an image I love.

Michael Hegerty, Diane and I decided to live permanently in Los Angeles. Chuggie had returned to Australia, as had KB and his band, and we became more estranged from Australia as the weeks grew into months. Chuggie would call and suggest coming home, but we were now comfortable with Merv Goldstein and Peter Burke and had started to network around the LA scene. Rick and Michael were earning good money playing in various bands around LA and I was feeling very much at home.

I had a meeting with Clive Davis, the industry immortal who had discovered Aretha Franklin, Paul Simon and many others. Clive was staying in a bungalow at the legendary Chateau Marmont—aka the 'Hotel California'—and Merv dropped me off with my guitar, on Clive's request, and directed me to the bungalow. I sat nervously in the elegant living room; Clive was on the phone in the bedroom. When he finally made his grand entrance, all he wore was a very elegant, expensive dressing gown, so short it could have been a gentleman's smoking jacket. Way too much of Clive was exposed.

Okay, I thought to myself.

'Play some of your songs,' he requested.

This would have been a perfectly good idea except for Clive's constant interjections. He happily told me he did this with all his acts; in fact, he'd just dumped a major act from Arista who failed to follow his musical directions. The poor bastards. I wasn't stupid and was less than impressed by Clive Davis, as famous as he was. I left the bungalow feeling rather indifferent about the whole thing.

Merv was waiting for me in the lobby with an old friend of his, Don Adams—yes, that's right, Maxwell Smart, Agent 86, the TV star. We had drinks and a hilarious ride home with Don, who was the living embodiment of his alter ego. He was incredibly funny. He kept asking me deliberately inane questions about Australia and, I suspect, cocking up Australia's geography. Imagine having that conversation with Maxwell Smart and you'll understand how funny it all was.

Money started to become a real problem by mid-1979. Something of a cold war broke out between Goldstein and Chugg, leaving us all in a very uncomfortable position. Chuggie returned to LA and invited Diane and me up to our favourite spot, an A-frame holiday house on Big Bear Mountain, just south of LA. It was snowing and Chuggie seemed in an especially affectionate mood. I'd soon find out why.

I became 'Rich' and he became 'Chuggo' and I felt myself getting suckered once again. After a bit of a drinking session, 'Chuggo' thrust a contract at me. It was an arrangement with Zev Eizik, a Melbourne promoter. The plan was for me to do a short but lucrative tour of Australia, a high-profile run of dates, with a guaranteed profit of 100 grand. I was tired, a little drunk—and broke—and reluctantly agreed.

I was going back on the road.

As I began to audition back-up singers and guitarists, I realised just how awesome LA really was. It was a musical Mecca. Merv lined up the finest female singers for me, all these amazing women, including Claudia Lennear (who'd been on Joe Cocker's Mad Dogs and Englishmen tour) and the two women from The Babys, who'd just had a smash with the song 'Isn't It Time'.

Somehow, they were all ready, willing and able to come to Australia with me for just $A150 per week.

As tempted as I was, I decided to take a different approach, and hired Chris Pinnick, an LA native who'd played guitar on 'Ace of Hearts' on my album and would soon join Chicago, and a well-known sax player. Diane would stay as back-up singer, just as she'd done back in Australia.

We fitted out the garage and began daily rehearsals. I continued to write and also did a bit of recording on a primitive four-track machine.

Very reluctantly, we all began to pack up the house and prepare for the long journey home. It may well have been the worst move that I have ever made.

15

'Don't you step in dark spaces,
Don't you go drifting into strange places'

Dark Spaces

Arriving back in Australia in winter 1979 felt very strange. Chuggie put us into a hotel in Macleay Street, Potts Point, and we were introduced to 'Scrooge' Madigan, our tour manager, who I suspect was employed more to look after Eisek's and Chugg's interests than ours. On the advice of Michael Hegerty and Diane, I set up a company called Gypsy Music. The three of us were directors.

Chris Pinnick, the American guitarist, became a rare highlight on one of the most traumatic tours of my life. He'd never set foot outside LA before, and quickly decided all Aussies were 'bozos' (as in the clown). Just shows how tolerant we are—the reverse would get you killed in the States.

Thankfully for good ol' Chris, not only did he get away with his outlandish behaviour but somehow he endeared himself to every Australian he met. Except for Scrooge, as it transpired.

After endless ribbing from the Australian contingent about dangerous crime in California, Chris would usually awake around midday with a big hangover, then bang on my door carrying a newspaper. Every day it seemed that Chris would find a story about a headless corpse in Sydney Harbour, or a torso in the boot of someone's car—ghastly crimes being committed right here in our home town.

I'd met the sax player in Los Angeles. I'd never worked live with a sax player, and I just didn't realise until he arrived in Sydney what a handful he was; he'd kept his bad habits well hidden back in the States. Now he was disappearing every night and zeroing in on the seediest haunts all over Kings Cross.

Chuggie decided to hire bodyguards, as the sax player was turning very self-destructive. But while two burly men guarded his hotel room door, he crawled down a drainpipe from many floors up and escaped back to the Cross. The man was out of control.

On the eve of my first sell-out concert at the Sydney Opera House, Chuggie convinced me to have my hair quite short and dress in an elegant white suit.

His intention was to promote me as a serious 'adult contemporary' artist, back from LA with a whole new persona. I went along with his plan.

The sax player seemed fine during the afternoon soundcheck; we all crossed our fingers, hoping the show would be problem-free. Indeed, the concert started in a very sophisticated fashion; everyone, including the sax player, behaved themselves impeccably. Yet somehow he managed to find drugs and booze somewhere. He bounded back out on stage about an hour into my very polite concert and started abusing the audience.

'C'mon—pretend you're all hippies and hold your hands above your head and clap your hands!' he yelled, berating the Opera House crowd.

I found the whole incident very embarrassing—I was a hippie and so was my audience. He was sent packing back to America the next day.

American singer/songwriter Tom Waits was at the Opera House show. I bumped into him backstage, a full bottle of Scotch in my hand. I moved to shake his hand but he grabbed the bottle instead, sculling the lot. Tom then proceeded to talk to me very articulately about how much he'd liked the show, about life, songwriting and the whole damned thing, without showing the effects of the bottle he'd just demolished.

The sax player wasn't the only drama I had to contend with on my return to Oz. I began a feud with Ian 'Molly' Meldrum. I'd never been a darling of the *Countdown* mob. I had no respect for the local pop marketeers; I just couldn't forgive them for feeding Australians a diet of pure pop candy and rejecting any music with credibility, intelligence and validity. Bob Dylan, Jackson Browne, Steely Dan and to a lesser degree, the Eagles, the Doobie Brothers and even Fleetwood Mac were given relatively scant regard by the *Countdown* mafia.

I think pop music is lots of fun, but watching *Countdown* was like going to the Easter Show and eating only fairy floss.

I may have had my disagreements with Festival Records, but they wielded a lot of power and *Countdown* was forced to accept me on the program. Reluctantly.

The band and I were staying at the Southern Cross Hotel in Melbourne and we were scheduled to appear on the show. We'd played a fantastic sell-out gig the night before and Chris Pinnick had had a huge night out. It was *Countdown* time and Scrooge the tour manager was losing patience trying to wake Pinnick. We arrived late for rehearsal, about 2 p.m.

Molly was waiting for me and launched into a tirade before I'd even located my dressing room.

'Who the fuck do you think you are?' he screamed at me. 'You're fucking fired, and we will never have you on this show again!'

I did my best to placate him. I agreed that we were less than professional being late for rehearsal and deserved to be axed from the show. I hoped that when this had all calmed down we could reschedule for a later date. But the more I tried to placate him, the more hysterical he became. I left the ABC studios thinking I'd never play *Countdown* again.

Just as I was leaving my hotel room that night, a journalist friend of mine, the music writer for the *Age*, phoned. He started pushing me for a comment on the drama.

'I just want to let sleeping dogs lie,' I replied. 'Let it go.'

I was late for the gig and finally, out of exasperation, I launched into a tirade of my own, a savage indictment of

Countdown. I challenged their right to ignore rock, a genre of music that had the biggest audience of all, bigger than pop, classical and others combined. *Countdown* virtually ignored all credible music. Unfortunately, my rant hit page two of the *Age*.

A short time later, Molly, to my surprise, asked to have me back on the show. When I arrived, Meldrum came out to greet me. He said he'd been very upset by the stories in the press and insisted that I owed it to him to do a live interview on that night's show. I resisted initially and, in the nicest possible way, suggested that any further aggravation would stir the tabloid press up even more.

Nevertheless, the Festival promotions manager coerced me into agreeing to the interview. I foolishly consented.

Meldrum and I spoke live to air and he launched into a strange rant—even though he intro'd me as 'a mate of mine'—while I unwittingly looked like a lamb being slaughtered. A million people watched this circus.

We disagreed about how late I was—I said 20 minutes, he insisted on 40—and then he brought up the press piece, insisting I only agreed to do the show 'because your manager ordered you to'.

'What *are* your feelings about *Countdown*?' he asked me.

'I'm not really sure,' I replied. 'That was a spontaneous remark that was made and I didn't expect it to be in the press. My attitude to everything that happened was to make it cool, calm and collected.'

Molly pushed me again about whether Chuggie forced me to do the show.

'I enjoyed doing the show,' I said, 'but there seems to be deep connotations about those events on the day. I wasn't even there when a lot of it occurred.'

It was all a bit of a pointless set-up. Molly ended by asking me to watch how the show handled my performance of 'Ace of Hearts', which I performed on set soon after, and come back and talk about it.

For weeks the tabloid press slashed into the *Countdown* myth with razor sharp cynicism. It was hardly a surprise that Molly and I never became especially close.

❖

We embarked on what should have been a short but busy tour. One night in Adelaide four of us were preparing to go and eat. Diane and I sat in the front of the rental car, Chris and Michael in the back seat. We were staying at a very seedy rock venue, the Arkarba, which had its own motel. Noddy, the lighting roadie, and Michael Wickow, the soundman, were staying in the room above mine.

Diane put the car into reverse and as soon as she touched the accelerator, there was a series of loud cracks. I had noticed a large number of people standing around the car park, but didn't think much of it. Now I realised they were police—we were in the middle of a shoot out! I looked up and saw Noddy come out of his room to see what was going on. Within seconds, the door near Noddy and Michael's room flew open and a masked gunman with a sawn-off shotgun charged out, barking obscenities at the cops.

Wickow rugby tackled Noddy and dragged him back into their room just as all hell broke loose. The police shot the first bad guy dead and he dropped over the balcony just like in the movies. A split second later a second Bandido flew out of the room. Suddenly, the Richard Clapton Band was caught in the crossfire.

I bolted around to the motel manager's office and screamed at him like a banshee; he told me that the cops had moved everyone to safety an hour earlier. Well, almost everyone. Finally, we made our escape in a taxi, but it had been too close for comfort.

Chris Pinnick, being a Hollywood native, was forever harping about the lack of drugs on the road.

'Whoever heard of a rock band with no drugs, you bozos!'

In the final stages of the tour we were to headline yet another huge outdoor hippie festival, this time in the northern NSW town of Byron Bay. As we pulled up, a roadie came running out to greet us and led us to our caravan. Somebody offered up some sort of exotic substance and that night, beneath a starry sky, Pinnick blew everyone away. I've since met people who insist it was one of the greatest gigs they have ever experienced. Then again, most of the 20,000 people in the audience were on some sort of substance or other and I'd guess that would have greatly enhanced their experience of the gig.

Sadly, things were beginning to go awry. I had Michael Hegerty and Diane on one side questioning the accounting and accountability of the tour, while Chuggie and Zev Eizik were insisting we add more dates because the tour was losing money. I was running out of patience; I still had opportunities back in Los Angeles. I had to get back there.

My allies in the local industry were telling me to forget America and pick up the pieces here. Merv Goldstein and Chuggie, meanwhile, had a particularly acrimonious falling out. Now I'd lost my American manager.

Diane and I found a flat in Vaucluse but kept it sparsely furnished. We wouldn't be staying long; we had to get back to LA. Michael Hegerty returned to America and we planned to regroup as soon as I could get the money owed to me from the tour. But it soon became apparent that I wouldn't be returning in a hurry.

I had befriended Andy Durant, from the band Stars, arguably one of Australia's best songwriters. Festival, meanwhile, was back in the mix, insisting that I record another album. I tried a couple of days recording with my old sparring partner Richard Batchens, but it just didn't work out. A short time later I met a guy named Mark Moffatt, who'd just started as Festival's in-house engineer, and he and Andy Durant served as the catalyst for me to remain in Oz and record the album that would become *Dark Spaces*, with me in my first role as producer. My production work on *Dark Spaces* was apparently the real reason that INXS wanted to work with me as their producer.

Andy had become depressed about the beast of an industry he found himself in, so he and I talked about forming a partnership. He moved up from Melbourne. I'd already written about an album's worth of material and was eager to co-write with Andy, something I'd never done before.

However, Andy just wasn't functioning most of the time. I couldn't tell if he was stoned or sick. The only time he seemed happy and functional was when he was hopelessly drunk on bourbon. I was scared to ask if he was using anything stronger.

Leglessly drunk, he and I went into Festival's studios and recorded a savage indictment against the music industry called 'Everybody's Making Money (Except Me)'. We played so loudly that the walls were shaking. That night Andy was throwing up every few minutes and I was getting very concerned. I had such respect and love for the guy that I really wanted to help him.

Andy headed back to Melbourne, moving in with his brother.

Not long after, Mal Eastick, the guitarist from Stars, called me.

'Andy's got melanoma. He's only got a couple of months to live.'

I was shocked. Andy was 25 years old. For the first time in my life I was faced with the Big Question. How was I going to deal with the impending death of a hugely talented and genuinely beautiful friend? What could I do to help?

Mark Moffatt and I continued working on the album under this strange dark cloud. I found solace in work, holing myself up in the studio where I'd spent so much time since 1972. I'd check in with Mal or Andy's family every couple of days, but I could feel him slipping away.

Back in the studio I stubbornly insisted that I wanted to use Kerry Jacobson, Dragon's drummer. To offset Kerry's wild ways, I employed Clive Harrison, arguably the father of all modern bass players in Australia. Every morning, Diane and I would get out of the house by 8 a.m. and begin our search for Kerry. Dragon had just been unceremoniously dumped by CBS; the record company had repossessed Kerry's drums and belongings. He was homeless and would latch onto a different girl every night at the Bondi Lifesaver.

The dilemma for Diane and me was where to start looking. We'd thump on doors until we found him. Invariably I would have to get Kerry to down some warm flat beer to get his day started. I would get him washed, try to feed him and then drag him off to the studio. Every morning Clive would be patiently waiting for us.

Clive was a Scientologist, a teetotaller, a bemused observer of rockers and their bad behaviour. Every morning, the greetings would play out like this.

'Morning, Kerry.'

'Morning, Clive, you shit bass player. Did you hear what I said, Clive? You are the shittiest bass player in the world. No, make that the known universe. No, make that the entire cosmos.'

Together, volatile Kerry and phlegmatic Clive made for an amazing rhythm section.

Despite all this apparent chaos, the album sessions were wonderfully creative; these intangibles gave the album its edge. We had hours of fun recording the song 'Dark Spaces', my first and only attempt to recapture some of the electronic experimentation I'd learnt all those years back in Berlin. We were also incredibly lucky to have American group The Fifth Dimension—known for hits like 'Up Up and Away' and 'Let the Sunshine In'—to do all the backing vocals under a pseudonym.

Mark taped the two Southern black girls talking about seeing 'Missy's mercy sake' under the table at a Thanksgiving dinner. (This curious phrase turned out to be slang for vagina.) Mark and I laughed our guts out. It was a hell of a story.

Dark Spaces was released in August 1980 and was yet another example of a record of mine being loved by the critics but failing to set the charts on fire. The reviews were probably the best of my career, and sales were ultimately pretty good, but only because I formed a great new band, under the management of Peter Rix (who's worked with Marcia and Deni Hines and Jon English), and built up a very strong live following.

I somehow managed to convince Kerryn Tolhurst, from the Dingoes, to join; we played together for a couple of years. Along with Mark Meyer on drums, the band had a spirited Stones-y/Black Crowes kind of vibe. Chris Copping, who'd played with the English band Procul Harum, was my keyboard player. This was the beginning of a fantastic run that sustained me throughout most of the eighties.

16

'"i am an island", some sucker scrawled,
"i am an island" on a city wall'

i Am an island

Andy Durant died on 6 May 1980. On 19 August, the famous Andy Durant Memorial Concert was staged in Melbourne. It was a profoundly sad event. Sure, there was much bravado and camaraderie between all the crew and the artists—the guys from Stars, Renée Geyer, Jimmy Barnes and many others—who presented the concert, but because of my relationship with Andy, I found it all incredibly difficult.

I'd never before had to confront death so directly, so profoundly. I kept hiding from the others; I felt strange and disoriented, constantly fighting back tears. I had to rationalise his death before I could learn Andy's songs. Being as obsessive as I am, it was simply too difficult to concentrate.

I don't know how I survived the gig. I was worried I might break down. By the time I actually made my entrance I was so nervous that I knocked over a chair and tripped on stage. I was dead sober, but so nervous I could barely function. To this day I can't watch the DVD of the show or listen to the live recording. It's just too hard, too painful.

❖

Out of the blue, my ex-manager Chris Murphy phoned and asked me to come and see him. He'd just begun to manage a new band called INXS, who'd recorded an album and were building a following.

'Come and check them out,' Murphy insisted.

But when he described their style of music and the nature of the band, and said he'd like me to think about producing them, I thought Chris had lost his marbles. When we'd worked together, Chris and I were into Neil Young and Bob Dylan; I couldn't believe he was asking me to take an interest in a new wave band, a style of music to which I couldn't relate.

Chris was as insistent as ever, however, and I reluctantly turned up at the Paddington Green Hotel at one o'clock in the morning to see this band of hairdressers. When I walked into the venue, I found that aside from Chris and his business partner Michael Browning, the crowd comprised about nine middle-aged drunks who were there because it was the only place to get a beer after midnight.

The band came leaping out on stage as if it was Wembley Stadium and my mood changed. I was bowled over by their enthusiasm and passion. They played a song called 'On a Bus' which was almost pure Steely Dan. For such young guys they were great players, and I was swept up by their awesome power. By the end of the set I was a convert and met the guys, gushing praise. Much to my surprise, I learned that their influences were not wildly different to my own. We forged an immediate rapport.

I was in.

We agreed to go into the studio and try recording one song together, a sort of test run. The band had decided they wanted to record a cover version of the old Loved Ones song, 'The Loved One', a hit from the mid-1960s. I jumped right in.

Conditions in the studio weren't really ideal, but the band was inspiring to work with, wildly enthusiastic. They made my production work a dream. There was no hint of negativity; everyone was focused, knew exactly where they wanted to go and were fiercely committed.

So why was I there? They needed the type of experience and information that I had access to, that I'd learned over the course of the previous decade. The one-day session played out like a dream, and I was asked to produce their second album. So began my high times with INXS.

Nineteen-eighty was one of the most eventful years of my life; I was involved in so many different things, although forging a career in America was placed on hold. I was a new man, trying to give up cigarettes, drugs and drinking and pursue the Taoist philosophy. I jumped head first into tai chi/kung fu classes.

I was approached by Mark Opitz to leave Festival, after eight years and eight albums, and sign with WEA Records. I had met Mark through Jimmy Barnes and Cold Chisel; he'd just landed the job as head of A&R. Mark had a brilliant strategy, to sign one act at a time. He signed Cold Chisel and then when they reached a certain level of success, he signed Billy Fields, who sold lots of records, and kept up this approach, signing Swanee and the Divinyls and then yours truly.

Opitz was undoubtedly the hippest producer of the early eighties; to be in with him was to be part of the most elite gang in Australian rock'n'roll. I had no hesitation in signing a three-album deal, believing it would help me build an American career without having to leave Australia.

As far as I'm concerned, this was the beginning of the greatest period of Oz Rock. It was all happening. The Divinyls were hot, acts like Midnight Oil were just starting to hit the gas. Venues like the Manly Vale and Royal Antler and Bombay Rock and the Venue in Melbourne were bursting at the seams. Millions of dollars were flying every which way; the industry was partying on cocaine and French champagne and trashing shiny new five-star hotels.

Mark Opitz, his girlfriend Vicky, Jimmy Barnes and his partner Jane moved into a big house in Brown Street, Paddington; the atmosphere reminded me of Chelsea in 1968.

Peter Rix and Chris Murphy planned a fairly long tour with INXS as support. The gigs went great; my audience responded really well to INXS. Their drummer Jon Farriss and I did tai chi every morning.

But INXS had no money. My band and I were staying at the Old Melbourne, a four-star hotel, while they were at Macy's, a real dump, sleeping virtually on top of each other and fighting off the roaches. While in Melbourne we were to shoot a live-to-air recording at Bombay Rock for the TV program *Nightmoves*, a very grown-up contrast to *Countdown*.

I arrived at soundcheck that afternoon to find a distress message from INXS's Kirk Pengilly, saying that Premier Artists, my booking agency, had replaced INXS with the Goanna Band. I spat the dummy and tried desperately to contact Peter Rix, but he avoided me all day. There were also problems with the road crew; suddenly this happy train was coming off the rails. That night after the gig I drank myself into a complete stupor, and the next day Rix and I parted company. It was time for a new start.

Tour manager Neil Wright looked after both INXS and me. The last gig of the tour was in Kempsey on the NSW North Coast and it was party time. At the end of the night I asked INXS to come back on stage and we did a couple of songs together. The place was going nuts. Michael Hutchence was very out of it and proposed an idea.

'Let's give the crowd a brown-eye.' (For the uninitiated, that involves dropping your strides and exposing your anus.)

The lighting guy threw the room into blackness and then threw a 'follow' spot on Kirk Pengilly, who was naked save for Kerryn Tolhurst's coat. Kirk threw open the coat and did his very own full monty. Then both bands went on stage in the darkness and assembled themselves into a straight line. Hutch and I stood at the front of the stage, jeering and laughing, while a group brown-eye was thrown.

But that wasn't the end of it. Michael grabbed the microphone and invited any keen young chicks in the audience to get on stage and flash their vaginas. I'm pretty sure that a few willing nymphets lifted their dresses and dropped their panties. Or did I just imagine that? Anyway, there was a riot.

Neil Wright was in a panic; he screamed that the police were on their way. Some people in the entourage were in possession of illegal substances, so getting out of there was a good idea. Both bands went screaming back to the motel and hightailed it out of Kempsey with a contingent of police and parents chasing us. It's said that no rock band ever played Kempsey again. Definitely not INXS, that's for sure.

I had been writing well, but became a little distracted by my studio work with INXS. It slowed down my songwriting, which was embarrassing because I had negotiated such an excellent deal with WEA and was expected to deliver a quality album.

Cold Chisel guitarist Ian Moss started coming around to my flat in Vaucluse and attempted to write with me, but these 'sessions' usually ended up as drinking binges with Mossy blazing away on guitar at 5 a.m. One day I went down to the communal washing line to apologise to my hard-working neighbours Helen and Bill. Helen was a schoolteacher, Bill an accountant clawing his way up the corporate ladder. I knew they woke up around 6 every morning.

I was apologising profusely when Bill stopped me.

'Wasn't that Ian Moss?' he gushed.

'Yes,' I replied and started my apology all over again.

'I'm honoured to be woken up by Mossy,' Bill confessed.

I found out that Bill had courted his wife at the Bondi Lifesaver, and he hated having his soul sucked dry by the corporate world. He said my nuthouse was like an oasis of dreams. I lived in the flat in Vaucluse for about seven years and Bill and Helen were treated to an endless parade of my friends.

I was trying to write an epic ballad about the history of Bondi. Being a child of Bondi, the trams and stories about the famous eccentric Bea Miles and the images you'd see of the suburb were ingrained in my memory. I had tentatively titled the song 'Bondondo Rondo', in honour of a block of flats in North Bondi.

Back in LA, Michael Hegerty was playing with a band of Mexicans. After a wild night in Pasadena, Michael called me at 3 a.m. on Australia Day and started raving sentimentally about 'the good ol' days of Bondi and the Lifesaver'.

The very autobiographical 'The Best Years of Our Lives' then came to life.

Having spent a great deal of time struggling with the original lyrics, the new, improved words poured out of me, thanks to Michael.

Mark Opitz and I originally thought it would be great if Cold Chisel agreed to be the band on my album. This made perfect sense; Mark was Jimmy Barnes's best friend, and their A&R man and producer, and I'd been hanging out a lot with Ian Moss.

As fate would have it, however, Chisel scored the support on Ted Nugent's American tour. I eventually persuaded Mark to let me have a go with INXS. They were definitely 'flavour of the month'—'The Loved One' reached the Top 20 and hits followed with 'Stay Young' and 'One Thing'—but they were a relatively untested unit in the studio.

However, Mark agreed to at least give it a trial run, and this part of Australian rock history was set in motion, pretty much by default. It also changed the entire artistic course of my career, and definitely made *The Great Escape* the interesting album that it is.

I was really pleased with quite a few songs on the album. 'I Am an Island' was written out of sheer stubborn tenacity. Hard rock songs are not really my forte, but I desperately needed an epic rock'n'roll blast to end my live sets. I laboured over that song for many weeks, sitting there with a primitive drum machine playing the feel over and over until I finally cracked the magic riff.

The lyric is my satirical take on the Darlinghurst art school set. I'd seen a piece of graffiti on a wall near the school; it read 'No man is an island'. With perverse glee, I turned the whole thing around, taking a sardonic view of pseudo-intellectual plagiarists. Another song, which also took ages to come together, was 'The Universal'.

But the most curious song on the album was 'Flow in Motion'.

In early 1982 I was determined to start getting my spiritual house in order. I began buying books on Taoism, and began tai chi classes every week. Jon Farriss was living with a tai chi instructor, and Jimmy Barnes and Mossy were also very enamoured with all things Oriental, especially Taoist and Buddhist philosophy. 'Flow in Motion' was my creative response to this newfound philosophy.

When we came to record the song, Mark Opitz was having problems with his girlfriend and split for a couple of days, leaving Jon, bassist Garry Gary Beers and myself in Sydney's Paradise Studios with Dave, the assistant engineer. We ran amok. We had food fights in the rec room upstairs and Garry stripped off to record nearly naked. I filmed the lot.

Madness aside, this was the most creatively free environment I've ever worked in. We would just sit around the studio and start playing when we felt like it and Dave would roll tape. 'Flow in Motion' was the result of wild experimentation and equally wild ideas. Jonnie was crucial, as was Ian Moss, who also joined us in the studio.

Also in Paradise Studios was the last manifestation of Sherbet, who were recording their final material. In an impetuous moment their guitarist Harvey James abandoned ship and joined my album and my band, Mossy by this time having left for the States. Harvey played most of the guitars with the studio band, until Mossy returned earlier than expected and added some fantastic parts of his own all over the record.

Paradise was like a music factory—Mark Opitz was producing both my album and a new Chisel album, while members of Chisel were playing with me. Jimmy Barnes sang backing vocals on 'I Am an Island' and Don Walker played on 'I Fought the Law'. Within a couple of weeks of Mossy's return my album was finished.

Mark Opitz proposed calling the album *The Great Escape*. At first I thought it was a little corny, and there was that Steve McQueen movie of the same name. The term was a throwaway line in 'The Universal'; to me it was another term for dropping out of society. I thought it through and figured that if I compromised and went along with the proposed title, then I could ensure that the cover image reflected my real meaning, capture more of a Byron Bay-hippie vibe.

Philip Mortlock was the guy in charge of art and graphics, and I spent some idyllic weekends at his weekender in

Kurrajong, kicking back while taking a plethora of photos with Roger Scott, all with a quasi-surreal feel. (Roger was married to Christine Hegerty.) We drifted for a while, not coming up with the perfect image. Mark started to apply some pressure and we decided that the cover image would be bright and colourful, not quite in synch with my original concept.

Again I thought it through. I'd spent much of the past decade arguing with my last record company, which hadn't helped my career. I truly believed in the quality of my work, and wanted my songs to be heard by as many people as possible. Being belligerent about an album cover wasn't going to help make this happen. Ultimately, I went along with everything the new record company wanted to do, much to their shock. The *enfant terrible* they'd heard about was suddenly Mr Nice Guy.

The people who worked at WEA Records in the early 1980s were, in my opinion, the best collection of people to ever work for an Australian record company. I truly respected them. The end result was that *The Great Escape* remains one of my biggest selling albums. The irony was that the record was sometimes much darker than even *Dark Spaces*, but clever marketing camouflaged this. The album reached gold status within a couple of months of its release in early 1982.

There was an interesting back-room drama. Cold Chisel had a band meeting and for whatever reason, their manager decided that Chisel's musical contributions should be erased from the tapes and all mention of the band erased from the cover. But the cover had already been printed and the album manufactured—this was a huge heart-stopper for me.

Were it not for the intervention of WEA's chairman Paul Turner (a gruff old bloke nicknamed The Dog), it would have been a disaster. A compromise was reached that Mossy, Jimmy and Don's work would remain on the album but all mention of them would be erased from the album's cover. I was obliged to keep this secret for some time, at least until Jimmy spilled the beans one night on *Nightmoves*.

I bumped into Mossy just after he'd read the *Rolling Stone* review of *The Great Escape*, which mistakenly gushed with praise for Harvey James's guitar playing. Mossy was pretty grumpy that he'd never be credited with what we all feel is some of his best playing.

My own record done, I wanted to get started on the INXS album. I made it known that I needed Alex Vertikoff, the American engineer from *Hearts on the Nightline*. Chris Murphy was in partnership with Michael Browning (ex-manager of AC/DC) and together they'd formed Deluxe Records. Deluxe was a low-budget operation, quite a contrast to WEA's spare-no-expense approach for *The Great Escape*. I foolishly agreed to $2000 in advance and $2000 on completion of the INXS album, but asked for a relatively high 3 per cent royalty.

I was obsessed with INXS and was beginning to spend more time on their project than promoting my own. We were going out a lot and partying; I revelled in their youthful decadence.

The first official session was at a pokey little rehearsal studio in the centre of Sydney. Michael Hutchence was fashionably late, and Andrew Farriss turned up with a cassette full of musical ideas. Listening to Andrew's tape, I wondered how I was going to transform it into an album of songs. They were really just abstract vignettes.

While Andrew and I debated this, Jon started bashing away at the drums, then Tim joined in on guitar and the rest of the band started jamming. Michael appeared and began singing nonsensical words. I stopped talking to Andrew and stood there, astounded at how this song came pouring out of them. Soon enough, with just a little help from me, 'Stay Young' was born. Too easy!

Michael was living in Kirribilli with his girlfriend Vicky—a model, of course—and we would have our meetings there. At our first meeting, Hutch was having trouble with his broken down old tape player and asked me to fix it. I had a look, but it was too technical for me.

'Sorry, mate, I can't help you,' I told him.

'I thought you were a record producer!' snorted Michael.

We all cracked up.

'Michael,' I had to ask, 'what do you think a record producer actually does?'

I think Hutch had 'record producer' confused with 'electronics engineer'.

I asked the band to bring a couple of favourite records around to Michael's so we could have a think tank—they brought in everything from Roxy Music to *My Life in the Bush of Ghosts*, a sort of urban sound collage produced by Talking Head David Byrne and Brian Eno. Out of this emerged the INXS sound.

Alex Vertikoff arrived from LA and moved in with Diane and me. On the first day of recording at EMI Studios in Sydney we were all excited; the loonies were about to take over the asylum. INXS might have been penniless, but their attitude was fantastic.

Every day Alex and I bounded into work full of energy and busting to get into this INXS record. There was the occasional domestic bickering, which can happen with three brothers in a band—but even the bickering was fun!

I enjoyed playing producer and running a tight ship, and mostly kept everyone away from the temptation of drugs and alcohol. As it was, Andrew would get very grumpy about anyone being out of it in the studio.

As a trade-off for all this good behaviour, I promised a huge party night in the studio, with girlfriends, when we recorded the title track 'Underneath the Colours'—but only if everyone would stay straight for the serious recording days. Everyone duly had a wild time, but we were all a bit too out of it and nearly didn't get the track down at all.

I had two days left to record Michael's vocals, over the course of a weekend. Michael was extremely nervous and couldn't perform to anyone's satisfaction, even though the building was empty. We tried everything. We ran an absurdly long cable to remote parts of the building—all over the place, in fact. I tried to become invisible, but he was freaking himself out. Nothing worked. I guess I'm one of the few people outside the band who witnessed firsthand just how emotionally and psychologically fragile Michael was. He simply had no confidence in his musical ability.

I pledged to Hutch that I'd tell Michael Browning we needed an extra $10,000 to hire Paradise Studios and record his vocals in the 'live' room, which had an ambience like a shower recess. It was the only place he felt comfortable.

Alex and I met with Browning at his office in North Sydney. As soon as I arrived, Browning took me aside and told me to abandon the INXS record and produce a heavy metal band for him instead. I declined. He duly launched into a rant about his credentials of working with AC/DC and that he knew a successful act when he heard it. His new heavy metal band was going to be world famous. And I was a loser for not recognising this.

'Michael,' I snapped back, 'INXS are going to be the biggest band in the history of Australian music. You're the one that doesn't know shit from shinola.'

When he asked me to leave, I asked for the $10,000 to finish the INXS album. Browning picked up his phone and hurled it at my head. Luckily, his aim was off. I was unaware that he and Murphy had had a dramatic falling out the week before—that was the background to our ridiculous argument. Murphy intervened, and I got the $10,000, took Hutch into Paradise and successfully recorded his vocals and mixed the album. *Underneath the Colours* was ready to roll.

17

'Whatever happened to the days way back (when) the Bondi Lifesaver was always raging'

The Best Years of Our Lives

There was a real buzz happening around my album *The Great Escape*, which was high on the charts. I needed to get back on the road, my second home. I assembled a band around Harvey James, with Mark Meyer on drums, Cos Russo on keyboards and Mary Bradfield on vocals. Bassist Graham 'Thommo' Thompson had just left Broderick Smith's band in Melbourne, and agreed to play with me, so I invited him to stay with us. We went into rehearsal and then straight into a video shoot for 'I Am an Island'. I was madly busy.

At the insistence of WEA Records I also took on a new manager, another whose identity I'd prefer not to reveal. Although the tour was very successful in terms of audience numbers, we seemed to be losing money like a leaky bucket. I'd made the band a proprietary limited company, with each band member sharing equally in the profits, which, thanks to this guy, eventually left us $60,000 in the red.

We started the tour playing to full houses everywhere, but bleeding money. Chris Bastic (later the Mayor of Randwick) came on board as tour manager and he really saved my sanity, because this spiral of debt dragged on for months.

I was beginning to live very excessively because I couldn't cope with the pressure of the debt. My grand plan for 1982 had been to buy a house, but that quickly went up in smoke.

The Great Escape tour wasn't all bad. The band played with loads of soul and there were lots of funny moments. En route to Melbourne for the hundredth time, the highway patrol pulled us over. Chris Bastic was driving and the police ran a routine check on him. They found $2500 worth of outstanding fines in his name, and hauled him off to jail. We were in a no-horse town, seemingly a million miles from anywhere.

This led to a major blow-up with my new manager. We needed a hefty amount of money to bail Chris out, and were running late for that night's show in Melbourne. It took hours to find the guy and talk him into going to his local police station in Melbourne to pay the bail. It was a pretty simple request but it took forever. We barely made the sold-out gig.

Still, life on the road had its pleasures. At the Old Melbourne Hotel, I was partying with a girl in my room and made three trips downstairs to ask one of the other band members if he wanted to join us. At 1 a.m., a very pretty girl wearing only a bath towel answered his door; at 3 a.m. a different but equally pretty girl, also wrapped in a towel, answered the door. At 5 a.m. a third girl answered the door; she was naked. I never did find out if he was entertaining all three at the same time.

Harvey James and I went AWOL in Byron Bay and awoke in a hippie commune, way off the beaten track. I'd passed out in the back seat of the rental car still fully clothed, wearing a heavy leather jacket, with my long hair dirty and matted. I found Harvey inside a shack with a number of hippies; they were still comatose. I wandered through dense scrub in a daze and came across the most idyllic mountain stream. I stripped off my clothes and plunged into the beautifully clean water. I didn't care that it was freezing. It was like having God come down to bathe my sins away.

Then I heard noises. I looked around, and half a dozen beautiful, naked, giggling hippie girls plunged into the stream, with Harvey in hot pursuit. Harvey and I lay back in the water with these incredible women splashing around us and swore that we would never leave. And we very nearly did stay.

Just before reaching Port Macquarie on the NSW North Coast, I was snoozing in the back seat when Thommo was pulled over for speeding. Harvey had been given this evil-smelling pot back at the commune; the rental car reeked. I came to and looked at myself in the rear vision mirror. I still looked like shit.

But Thommo was in real trouble, and Harvey certainly wasn't helping, so I made a concerted effort to get out and make my presence known. The cop was stunned.

'Richard Clapton!'

He simply couldn't believe that he was booking my band.

'Me and my brother are your biggest fans,' he raved. 'We grew up on your music.'

He told us he'd be happy to rip up his paperwork and forget the whole thing, but only if we agreed to have dinner at his brother's restaurant that night. I agreed in a heartbeat. Talk about The Great Escape.

But the tour dragged on, as long and money-bleeding tours tended to do. By the time we reached Selina's in Sydney, my band had started to get distracted, too. Harvey brought along a small black and white TV and placed it on a chair on his side of the stage.

At soundcheck, I spoke with the roadies.

'What's with the TV?'

They had no idea.

That night, in front of 2000 people, I bounded on stage, only to see my guitarist with his eyes glued to a TV set.

Between songs, I shouted at him over the noise of the crowd.

'What the fuck are you doing, Harvey?'

'Ralph,' he yelled back, pointing at the screen, 'it's the FA Cup!'

I'd forgotten just how loyal a Pom Harvey really was. He spent the night both playing his heart out *and* watching the soccer.

Despite our boozing, we maintained a consistently high playing standard. In a strange way, the booze enhanced the great emotional depth of the band and the songs. The venues started filling up again.

But a rift started to grow between Harvey and me. One night in Tasmania, Harvey began gesturing at me on stage, making 'rabbit ears' behind my back as I was playing 'Goodbye Tiger'. Bad move. I exploded. As soon as we came off stage I started hurling chairs and anything I could lay my hands on at him. It was an ugly scene. I fired Harvey and then the whole band threatened to quit. Frankly, we'd all had enough.

A new tour manager named Tom Keogh somehow kept my sanity, and the band, intact. He even managed to control the excessive drinking and occasional drugging.

I had parted ways with Diane quite some time before and met a beautiful girl in Melbourne. Typically, I was instantly besotted with her. I moved into her rented house in Melbourne; being on the outskirts of the city, away from the 'scene', probably kept me from having a nervous breakdown.

But she was inclined to get very drunk to mask her shyness. At one of the leading venues in Melbourne, she got so drunk she actually curled up and went to sleep undetected. When the gig ended there was no sign of her. I frantically searched everywhere and was aghast to find her curled up beneath the bass bins, the huge speakers on the bottom of the PA.

I played Selina's in the Sydney suburb of Coogee. Bob Dylan was in town and a friend of mine who knew Dylan well had introduced him to my music, from *Goodbye Tiger* onwards. The word went out that Dylan would come to see me play. I had a full house and the gig was going really well, but I kept running over to the side of stage to ask if anyone had spotted Dylan.

'Where's Dylan?' I shouted. 'Is he here yet?'

The show ended and after numerous encores I still couldn't confirm whether Dylan made the gig.

I wasn't told the truth until afterwards. Dylan had in fact turned up at the front door, with an entourage of a dozen people.

Some genius bouncer said to Dylan: 'I don't give a flyin' fuck who yer are, mate, yer not comin' in 'ere with all yer fuckin' hangers on! So fuck off!'

Another golden opportunity blown—and not through any fault of mine.

Late in what seemed like a never-ending tour, Chuggie began appearing at gigs and bringing me gifts to lure me away from my manager. He didn't need to work too hard; despite our chequered history, Chuggie was a dream compared to the other guy. I moved back to Sydney, along with my girlfriend, who got a job in radio.

Chuggie looked at the books and had to break it to us that we were deeply in debt. Fortunately, because we had the touring company well set up, we just went belly up and liquidated it.

Women, as you've probably noticed by now, have always been great stabilisers for me, and my girlfriend and I quickly and happily set up house. She was an urban hippie and brought out all those good characteristics in me. She calmed me down, coerced me into a healthier lifestyle, at least enough to curb the self-destructive tendencies I had lapsed into.

I had been skirting around the fact that 'I could have been a contender' in America, but had probably missed my chance. But now it really hit home. And with the combination of Diane and me parting ways and Andy Durant's death, I became uncontrollable. But instead of diving headfirst into the nightlife, I poured what money I had into new equipment for my home studio. I also began to write again, songs that I felt were among my best.

Chuggie didn't push me too hard, having learned from past mistakes, and I developed a positive attitude to work. Unfortunately, the staff at WEA had changed a great deal since *The Great Escape*. The new A&R man and I didn't have a great rapport.

I realised that he had very little empathy with my music, and treated what was the most serious factor in my work—the songs—as an excuse to call meetings and get wasted.

To make matters worse, he began using me as a pawn to lure INXS to sign with WEA. Consequently, I became disenchanted with the label, as did Chuggie.

The crunch came when Chuggie and I met with the A&R guy and asked for $10,000 to record a video for 'The Best Years of

Our Lives'. We were bluntly turned down. This outraged Chugg, who was not going to accept rejection from this newbie. Mid-sentence, Chuggie spotted someone higher up the WEA food chain, and locked into stride with him.

The two disappeared into the executive bathroom. In less than five minutes, Chuggie returned to the A&R office and gave me the nod.

'Cool,' he jubilantly exclaimed, 'we've got our budget.'

But our time with WEA was running out. I left and moved to Mushroom Records.

18

'Now I'm sitting here trying to make
some peace within my mind,
With the late movie flickering back
and forth across my eyes'

Katy's Leaving Babylon

In 1983 I was recruited into The Party Boys, a so-called 'supergroup', a really popular live act. From the outset, this band was, as the name implied, the hardest-living group of musos in Australia. Talk about the party that never ended.

My first night with them took place at Tharen's, a very upmarket restaurant in Darlinghurst. EMI Records was hosting the night; the band's first album had just gone gold. What could have been a great meal was left untouched while band and label raised hell. We then moved on to James Reyne's room at the Sebel Townhouse—I was filling in for James in the band—and proceeded to trash it, doing silly rock star stuff like pulling paintings and mirrors off the walls, tossing things around, just wreaking havoc.

At the first rehearsal, I arrived and patiently waited for the rest of the band—Kevin Borich, Harvey James, bassist Paul Christie and Angels' drummer Graham 'Buzz' Bidstrup—who eventually arrived several hours late and then proceeded to party on. Before I knew it we were on stage at the Manly

Vale Hotel, drunk as skunks and playing like maniacs to a full house.

I wasn't too enamoured with the band's music, which was all famous covers, because PC, the band demagogue, would insist everything we played be transposed. Consequently, as James had warned me, I had to struggle with ludicrously inappropriate keys, which left me sounding either like Mickey Mouse or Satan. The tour ran for two long weeks, and although we each made fantastic money, to me it felt like artistic prostitution.

There are two very funny stories from this period, however, which should be recounted. During that first tour, Buzz Bidstrup (the Angels drummer) and I became good friends and maintained each other's sanity throughout all that pressure. One night Buzz and his wife Kaye invited me and Jimmy and Jane Barnes around for a small, intimate dinner party. Everyone was drinking fine and expensive wine, but unfortunately I have always been very allergic to the histamines in wine. Jimmy began ribbing me for not partaking but I stood my ground because I knew that pretty soon I would go red in the face and become very inebriated. Nevertheless, much to my chagrin, I allowed myself to be talked into having a few glasses of wine. Just as the wine was taking effect, I realised that it was unusually strong and immediately regretted drinking some. To make matters worse, Jimmy insisted we get stuck into the vodka.

Jimmy then produced a home video camera he had hidden away and methodically began setting it up on a tripod in front of me.

'Whaddya doin', Jimmy?' I asked, my brain turning to jelly.

Jimmy said nothing, then suddenly joined me on the lounge and introduced *The Jimmy Barnes Tonight Show*. My mouth was dry, and I could hardly speak. I just wanted to curl up and go to sleep.

Jimmy began doing takes of his *Tonight Show*, with me as his special guest, much to the hilarity of everyone else. Jimmy is actually fantastic at this stuff, and could very easily make a successful talk show host if he ever chooses that fork in the road. (He did have his own TV show in the new millennium.)

However, by this stage I was catatonic and we sat there doing take after take, with Jimmy intro'ing his show and me pissed out of my brain. The only words I could utter were: 'Whaaaaat are ya doin?', 'Why?', or 'Switch that fuckin' thing off, for Chrissake.' I guess you had to be there but it sure was funny at the time.

A certain guitarist came out on my next outing with The Party Boys. The guitarist was renowned for leaping off a PA stack at the Newcastle Workers Club, and during the ensuing solo, exposing himself to the audience. His nickname was The Beast.

I'd planned a return trip to Berlin straight after the tour. The tour ended in the rural NSW town of Taree; we all woke up quite late in a seedy motel. I had an impressive camera, complete with an expensive motor drive. I took about a dozen shots of the band, then forgot all about it.

I arrived in Berlin some weeks later. I'd completely forgotten the photo shoot in Taree. Volker and I went out soon after my arrival, and I finished the roll of film by shooting the old Gestapo HQ, the Reichstag and other prominent Nazi buildings that I thought might be demolished. I was very serious about the shots, taking light readings and being careful with my exposures.

I left the film with a laboratory close by the apartment where we were living. A young, pretty Berlin girl was working behind the counter and insisted on going through every shot with me to ensure that I was satisfied with the processing. She worked her way backwards through the shots of Berlin, diligently asking for my approval of the colours and exposures.

Then she burst out laughing, and asked me who this was in the first dozen frames.

'Oh,' I said nonchalantly, flashing back to Taree, 'you see, I'm a rock musician from Australia, and this is a band I play with called The Party Boys.'

'*Ach ja!*' she said, then proceeded to giggle.

In the band shots, The Beast was progressively rolling up his short shorts to reveal his penis in the last half dozen shots. Here I was, 20,000 kilometres away, trying to explain (in

German) about this amusing character, and how this wasn't common behaviour for Australian men.

❖

I'd decided to make a last-ditch effort to make some inroads in the German music scene. I moved back into Volker's apartment and renewed my old European contacts, and began making new ones. At first I seemed to be received remarkably well and it was all very exciting. One valuable ally was a Hamburg-based record company exec, a guy named Hans, who worked for Polygram. He loved my albums and pledged to put his full weight behind my European career.

I spent a lot of time in Hamburg and Amsterdam; people like Bruce Cockburn and J.J. Cale were popular throughout continental Europe and I fitted better there than in the UK. I assured Hans that if he helped me secure a deal, I'd focus strongly on Europe.

I set myself up in a wonderful little *pension* in one of the better areas of Hamburg, and started working the phones. After a couple of days, Hans phoned to tell me that after a long period of disenchantment with Polygram, he was so frustrated with the company that he'd quit. He had plans to set up his own independent company operating out of a recording studio complex in Hamburg. I was a little disappointed, but within the week he'd lined me up a meeting with his successor at Polygram.

It proved handy that Volker and Georgie had taught me 'street' German—it would come in useful during my sit-down with these industry goons.

The two very rude execs kept me waiting while they made insulting remarks—in German, of course—not just about Dragon, with whom they'd recently been dealing, but the whole Australian rock scene. I sat there feigning ignorance, while they giggled and tittered about how Europe would never take Australian music seriously. After another insulting remark about Dragon, I'd had enough, so I joined the discussion in German. They were startled and desperately tried to qualify their remarks. It was all a waste of my time.

I returned to my *pension* more despondent than victorious; the incident had rammed home to me what a low calibre of people ran the European music scene. I had similar experiences in Hilversum, the music capital of Holland, Paris and Munich. No one rated Australian music in any way, the fools. They had no idea. It wasn't as if the Europeans were breaking new ground in rock music; much of it was pretty bloody awful.

My old friends from the German rock scene were victimised by these BMW-driving deadshits and had to leave for England or America to build careers. Back in Hamburg, my friend Hans and his associates urged me to give it one last shot, but I was so angry I was longing to get home.

I returned via New York, with the intention of crashing out for a couple of months with Georg and Sabine. However, Georgie had changed a great deal since the late seventies. He'd worked on his English and could now communicate with his fellow New Yorkers. He and Sabine had moved up the social scale—frankly, I found the parties we attended a little bit intimidating. Sabine was hanging with an intellectual crowd, while Georg was mixing with architects and the arty crowd, who all seemed to be chasing young actresses. Once I would have found this scene cool, but I was weary of all the glamour and pretensions.

One night at one of these parties, there was all kinds of clandestine sexual activity going on. I needed to get the hell out of there and across to California, where I felt much more at home. Once again, Georgie was upset that I wanted to leave but I told him that I couldn't just divorce myself from Australia. I had to get home eventually.

John Brommell, my Australian publisher, was in LA so I made the excuse that we had some meetings planned. I only spent a short time with John, but was there long enough to be impressed at how he and Jane—his secretary—had succeeded in charming the pants off the Americans with their 'Aussie-ness'. John urged me to return to Australia, to record again.

'We'll have another shot here with the next album,' he assured me.

I headed home, but not before clearing my head in Hawaii for a couple of days. It couldn't hurt after what I'd just been through.

Before I'd left Australia, there was room to move in the local scene. But now there were really good quality bands playing in venues all over Australia—every night of the week. I'd never heard of Flowers or Mental As Anything or the Eurogliders, or countless other bands, but I soon discovered they were very fuckin' good! For the first time in my career, my agent had to worry about placing me in a venue in Sydney's suburbs, to put some distance between me and an equally good act who were scheduled to play elsewhere that night. The agency would have to book their acts at geographically different points.

A new explosion of great Australian music was spilling over onto the world markets. I reckon Sydney probably had more great talent per capita than New York. Rod Muir, who owned the Austereo network, which included the Triple M powerhouse, was running radio; he also had his fingers in TV rock shows. The amazing thing was that there was room for so many acts on radio and TV.

My new contract with Mushroom Records was not one of their more glamorous deals, but it offered enough for me to record a decent album. Chuggie sent me up to the Gold Coast for two weeks of intense songwriting. The only trouble was that every rock band in Australia seemed to be passing through the Gold Coast. The minder Chuggie had employed for me became bored and started handing out our contact details to anyone and everyone. I feared it becoming a fortnight-long rock'n'roll party.

We were visited by a couple of gorgeous Gold Coast groupies, desperately trying to escape the clutches of Sydney's most lecherous musician. Lucky old me, at least until lover boy turned up at the front gate of the luxury resort where I was staying. He didn't buy my lies and insisted on coming up to the apartment for a visit.

What transpired was an absurd comedy of errors. I knew of an obscure exit at the back of the building, which should have enabled us to flee undetected. Unfortunately, the other guy got horribly lost—when the doors of the goods lift opened into the dingy bottom basement, I came face to face with the playboy of the western world. Sprung!

Back in Sydney, the music industry gravitated to Benny's Bar in Potts Point like moths to a rock'n'roll flame. Every night this elite club was packed. Without naming names, let me simply say that everyone who was any kind of public figure (be they in radio, TV, sports, music, whatever) was a member of the club. There was always a tough guy on the door who knew how to separate the high-profile movers and shakers from the wannabes.

Without exaggeration, I'd estimate that a large portion of the day-to-day running of the music industry in the early 1980s was conducted in the booths and toilets of Benny's. And every major visiting rock star—from Elton John to David Bowie and Fleetwood Mac—just had to check the place out. There they'd be, holding court with their promoter and record company reps.

Probably the central figure at Benny's was Dominique, an expat Frenchman who ran the venue. The place was quite small, but the decor was perfect for a speakeasy. If you didn't feature in the photo display of owner Grant Hilton, which appeared on the wall of the club, you didn't figure in the scheme of things at all.

I was in Benny's when I was introduced to English band Duran Duran, who were recording an album in Sydney. I knew a strange friend of the band, who seemed to be a semi-permanent resident at the Sebel Townhouse, another industry place where there seemed to be no rules. We'd typically start the evening at either EMI or a restaurant, move on to Benny's round midnight, then end up in this guy's suite at the Sebel.

I was moving with another tribe altogether; it all seemed so unlike me. I still wonder how I managed to be hanging around with so many international celebrities. To be honest, this is embarrassing rather than a case of idle boasting; I really don't understand what the hell I was doing spending endless nights with people with whom I had little in common.

Dominique claims that one night he caught me inside the female toilet, cheering on while Michael Hutchence offered drugs to any woman who'd show us her breasts. Dom had to call a halt to our little game because Michael had a dozen girls queued up. Dom thought it was all getting a little out of hand.

I had an amusing night in the Sebel Townhouse bar with Glenn Shorrock and Elton John. We were making wagers on who'd had the closest brush with the law. Glenn romped home—he'd had some remarkable escapes.

Elton had been buying us top-shelf cognac as if there was no tomorrow, and we started to slur our words. Shorrock wisely decided to call it a night, leaving Elton and me to fly the flag. Before I realised it, the clock on the wall said 5 a.m., and I was also about to call it a night, when I noticed a beautiful blonde woman in a clinch with someone in a darkened corner of the tiny bar.

I pointed her out to Elton.

'Yeah, whatever,' he shrugged. 'It's just Cheryl Ladd snogging my drummer.'

What Elton didn't know was that I'd blab on endlessly about Cheryl Ladd to my girlfriend of the time just to give her the shits; Cheryl was the hottest of all Charlie's Angels. (Of course I'm joking!)

At this point the alcohol swept over me, and I lunged towards her and fell to my hands and knees.

'Cheryl Ladd! Cheryl Ladd!' I shouted. 'We're not worthy!'

She let out a snort and haughtily stepped over me and stormed out of the bar. I turned back to Elton but he too had slipped away. Talk about life's most embarrassing moments; this is the only time I've ever behaved like a complete arsehole with a celebrity. I swear.

19

'Hey kid! don't you lean on me,
i wanna talk to you, about Solidarity'

Solidarity

My professional life in Sydney gravitated around the Mushroom office, manned by Liz Dainey. I soon came to realise that Mushroom was a very Melbourne-oriented record company. Liz was rather a solitary soul in the Mushroom world; I was virtually her only Sydney act doing much. Gudinski would phone me quite frequently, but only to alert me to the fact that he was coming to Sydney to catch up. Liz was sharing an apartment with the actress Kate Fitzpatrick; there was a small but exclusive club of her friends, people like Rob Hirst from Midnight Oil and James Reyne, who'd frequent their little soirees.

Thanks to the advent of affordable home studio gear and things like drum machines, my songwriting flourished. I was able to realise my musical ideas without being undermined by extraneous factors. But I used the machines to write 'rootsy' music, rather than techno-funk, the current musical flavour. I wrote songs like 'Katy's Leaving Babylon' and 'Atom Bomb' *using the technology*, rather than it using me.

I began experimenting with these machines. I was lured into buying a sequencer and as soon as I got it home and hooked it up, I wrote a bass line, pressed play on the drum machine and out popped this tremendous feel, which conjured up images of Berlin.

Eastern Europe was changing; there was so much drama in the air. I still had a few close friends there; we spoke regularly. I found myself writing an album about Europe from the standpoint of a European. Songs like 'Solidarity', 'Amsterdam' and 'New World' came out in a torrent of creative activity.

I started recording in the $2500-a-day Rhinoceros Studios with Mark Opitz, who was impressed by the grungy guitar sound I'd captured on 'Solidarity'. He couldn't believe I could get that sound through the tiny 10-watt amp I used at home in Vaucluse. That bedroom guitar track stayed.

All this music and technology, however, was an escape for me. I was feeling insecure and unsettled, but rather than confront my demons, I left the real world behind and lived in an imaginary state within my own mind.

I chose to use Buzz Bidstrup on drums, who'd become my constant companion, and Graham Thompson on bass, plus an assortment of the best keyboard players. I'd play most of the guitars myself. Buzz had a much stronger personality than Mark and the album began faltering very early on. Buzz asserted his ideas and staked out his territory, whereas Mark became withdrawn. This was my introduction to David 'Chippa'

Nicholas, who engineered the album, which I named *Solidarity*. Not only did he save the album, but Chippa became one of my best friends and supported me through tough times.

I'd written songs about the imminent end to the Cold War, and ironically, there was a sort of 'cold war' at Rhinoceros for a couple of months in mid-1984. Opitz was rarely at the studio; I was freaking out that all my work would end up in the trashcan.

Inevitably, the mood turned dark and everybody started drinking as a panacea. It never works. We decided to shut down for a couple of weeks.

With only days before we were due back, Buzz, Chippa and I panicked. No one had heard from Opitz. We had the studio booked for a further month, but there was no producer, no plan. I jumped on the phone to assemble the best band I could. Along with Thommo and Buzz, I hired Mark Moffatt on guitar and Alan Mansfield from Dragon on keyboards.

I had just co-written a song called 'Kathleen' with Guy Delandro; I decided we'd start with that. We all arrived punctually at 10 a.m. and by 4 p.m. we had just about finished the track. Alan had a predilection for Scotch and had been having a few nips during the afternoon. He was sitting between Mark Moffatt and me on the sofa in the control room, ridiculing Opitz loudly and mercilessly.

A lone figure came slinking into the control room, sat hunched over the console, looking at the floor, not saying a word. Mansfield continued his diatribe and Moffat and I poked him in the ribs, pointing at the guy hunched over the console.

'Shut up!' we mouthed at him.

Al had drunk one too many Scotches and couldn't understand what we were on about. Opitz stood up and stormed out of the room. I chased him around to a vacant studio, where he admonished me for all kinds of things. I felt he was overreacting until he finally pointed out to me what had really pissed him off.

'All these musicians you have,' he said, pointing to my team, 'are accomplished record producers in their own right.'

I burst out laughing. He was right. I just hadn't thought of that!

That didn't improve the recording process. Chippa and I worked alone for the most part, but this was probably a good thing. Chippa's fantastic people skills brought out the best in my guitar playing. To finish the project, Chippa and I worked for 40 hours without any rest. I played guitar until my fingers literally bled. David and I were just about hallucinating, and thinking that the young cleaning lady was looking awfully good at 5 a.m.

I finished all the lead guitar on the track 'Amsterdam' by dousing my fingers in whisky, the pain was so bad. Other tracks were in a state of disarray. 'Cry Mercy Sister' had two different bass players playing two different things; the final mix shows the chaos that was going on. If you listen, there is actually a gap where one player's track takes over from the other.

The great Venetta Fields was rushed in to sing on incomplete tracks. Venetta was told she'd have to sing her backing vocal to a drum machine and a bass guitar on 'Feelin' Alright Tonight'.

'Try and imagine the keys and guitar,' she was informed.

Venetta crinkled up her brow with annoyance.

'Say what? I can't imagine nuthin', motherfucker! What the hell have you been doin' in here all this time?'

Good question.

Gudinski and Chugg were clamouring for a hit single. One afternoon they both burst into the studio to inform Opitz and me that I should record a 'contemporary' sounding single to help launch the album. Opitz said he wasn't too enthusiastic about this idea.

'Get another producer,' he told them.

Gudinski hired Mark Moffatt, as well as transplanted South African Rikki Fataar, who'd drummed with the Beach Boys and Tim Finn, and most recently Bonnie Raitt, and an American engineer called Tim Kramer. I had a rough idea for a song called 'The Heart of It', a very basic pop tune that could be adapted into a dance track. We recorded the song in one day. I have no hesitation in saying the song wasn't all that great, but Moffatt and Fataar really 'pulled one out of the box'; the 'feel' Rikki gave to the track was pure magic.

I heard this incredible drumming in my headphones while I was singing and looked back at Rikki, who seemed to be asleep while hammering out this steaming chunk of funk!

SOLIDARITY

I began hanging out with Tim Kramer quite frequently but had to pull back because he was caught up in a world of drugs from which he never did escape. Tim was a real human dynamo who'd stock up on drugs and work for days without sleep. Timmy lived in a dark Netherworld that I found a little too scary. He dreamed of meeting the girl of his dreams in Australia, but it never happened. Some time after he returned to America, he died. Roger Mason wrote 'Token Angels' as a tribute and captured Tim Kramer's tragic life perfectly.

I decided I needed a co-manager, and told Chuggie that I wanted to hire Warren Cross, who'd been my lawyer and INXS's for a time. This led to some comical situations on tour because Warren was still inexperienced in the music business.

We met back in 1980, when he was still at law school, a crazy fan who'd stand right down the front of the stage every night going troppo. He became a very valuable ally.

On the road, Warren was like a kid in a candy store. Touring was still a romantic sort of thing; not quite glamorous but very Jack Kerouac. An adventure. But our tour manager, whom I won't name, was a small-time drug dealer and the tour took on a very decadent character. (Years later the same guy was either pushed from, or fell out of, a high-rise window on the Gold Coast.)

❖

The feature of my live band was Venetta Fields with Shirley Mathews on backing vocals. They were two incredible women. Shirley wore rollerskates everywhere—she was quite a sight to behold in little Australian country towns, skating down the main street on the hunt for health food.

One day, in the back of a Greyhound bus Chuggie had hired to get us from Melbourne to a festival on the NSW Central Coast, I sat and listened intently to Venetta for something like 12 hours. She talked us through her incredible story: being an 'Ikette' for Ike and Tina Turner, working for years with Aretha Franklin, singing with Pink Floyd on the Dark Side of the Moon tour. Singing back-up vocals for Little Richard when Jimi Hendrix was his lead guitarist. Venetta also sang on virtually every Steely Dan and Boz Scaggs album.

'What was it like working for Van Morrison?' I asked her.

'I've never heard of him,' she replied.

I told her that I had a video of Venetta and Shirley singing back-ups for Van Morrison on American TV.

'No, I've never heard of him,' she insisted.

I described his physical appearance, but still failed to jog Venetta's memory. I told her the song titles and suddenly she remembered.

'Aw—hiiiiiiimmmm!' she all but screamed. 'Yeah, now I know—lights on, but nobody's home! My God! Was that Van Morrison? He is the weirdest person I ever met in my whole life!'

SOLIDARITY

Sometimes Venetta dozed off during this marathon session. We'd give her a nudge and she'd just pick up right where she'd left off.

We were playing a big outdoor show in Canberra with Midnight Oil; each act had their own tent. I took Venetta over to meet the Oils, but as I led her into their tent, she turned heel and ran off squawking. I ran after her, admonishing her for being impolite, but she said that Peter Garrett had scared the shit out of her.

'He's so big—and so white! And shit, man—he ain't got no hair!'

Suddenly the Chinese expression 'white ghost' made perfect sense to me.

❖

In the 1980s I consolidated many of the friendships I had formed with the weird and wonderful people in Australian radio. For years I'd been great mates with Peter Grace (who went on to produce Martin and Molloy), and had also befriended people like Charlie Fox, Billy Pinnell and Stan Rofe, as well as becoming a part of the Double Jay (or JJJ) family. My most enduring friends in radio over the years have been Doug Mulray, Stuart Cranney and Paul Holmes.

Paul Holmes and I were fixtures at Benny's. Paul had the most chequered but awe-inspiring career in Australian radio.

He was probably the original maverick bastard son of radio, the most loveable, rambunctious loose cannon ever foisted on the Australian public.

One night (probably more than one night, now I think about it), Holmesy was so drunk he'd fallen over in the gutter outside Benny's. It was about 5 a.m. and he was shouting any expletive that came into his head. Screaming at the world. Finally a police paddy wagon came rolling by. Paul began shouting abuse at the cops, calling them 'fuckin' pigs' and challenging them to arrest him. I walked over and nervously said the first thing that came into my head.

'It's okay, officers—it's just Paul Holmes.'

We were lucky that Holmesy was one of Sydney's most popular announcers.

'Oh, fine then,' they replied and rolled off down Challis Avenue.

Jimmy Barnes was scheduled to come down to my gig at the Ferntree Gully Hotel and sing 'I Am an Island' with me. Jimmy didn't show up and the gig ended. Venetta and I drank the entire supply of white wine from the backstage rider; I got really shitfaced. A chauffeur walked into the dressing room and told me that Jimmy had asked him to deliver me to his gig at the Venue in St Kilda.

SOLIDARITY

Despite my protestations the driver insisted, and dropped me off at Jimmy's gig. I sat in a tiny space at the side of stage, watching the band, visible to some sections of the audience. Between songs, Jimmy was running across and pouring vodka down my throat. Gradually, I just lost the plot altogether. I was so drunk I couldn't comprehend what was going on.

I heard Jimmy talking about his mate Ralph—as most people referred to me—and in my drunken stupor thought this was the cue for me to get up and sing with Jimmy. I struggled on stage, and stood there swaying. Jimmy didn't know I was there. When he finally turned around and saw me he yelled: 'Not now, Ralph, ya stupid cunt! Get off the fucking stage. I'll call ya up later!'

By now I was feeling humiliated and plain awful and just wanted to escape. Unfortunately, Michael Gudinski insisted that I couldn't leave until I'd joined Jimmy onstage for the encore. He set to work trying to sober me up.

Jimmy finally got me on stage and threw a guitar around my neck. This particular guitar, a Steinberg, has an unusual design, and as soon as I put it on it swung around behind my back. Jimmy asked me to start out the chords to Dylan's 'Like a Rolling Stone', but the guitar kept swinging around and around. I was still so drunk I was getting confused.

'Can someone get me a guitar?' I'd ask, even though the damn thing was on my back.

Jimmy repeatedly swung the guitar around, only for it to swing around again. And I continued asking for a guitar. Jimmy and I were doing our own Laurel and Hardy slapstick routine, the audience exploding with laughter. According to eyewitnesses, I stayed on stage long after Jimmy, winding the crowd up to chant for more encores. I don't recall a thing.

The next morning I woke up with the most depressing hangover and a serious bout of paranoia. I didn't have the nerve to phone Jim until late afternoon. When I did, I launched into profuse apologies. To my amazement, Jimmy kept assuring me that I'd been an asset to his gig. Everyone found the incident hilarious; really it was okay.

'Don't worry about it, Ralph.'

It was a great example of the camaraderie and unconditional bonds that I was lucky enough to experience in the Australian music industry.

In the eighties I'd elevated my entourage and myself to much classier establishments. For many years, the Southern Cross in Melbourne was like a second home. The incredibly tolerant night manager was the brother-in-law of one of Australia's iconic rock stars. I can't ever remember the hotel admonishing us for anything.

SOLIDARITY

A well-known and very Spinal Tap-like British band were partying loudly one night at the Southern Cross. They kept phoning room service, requesting that drugs be sent up to their suite. Finally, a waiter was dispatched with a room service trolley bearing a large silver plate covered by a silver dome. The party animals lifted the lid off the tray and found six neatly rolled joints and six lines of coke, just as they'd ordered. Now that's service.

A friend of mine, a guitarist with one of the biggest bands in the world, told me all kinds of stories about high times at the Southern Cross. His band all carried chainsaws housed in road cases, and after leaving large cash deposits with the hotel management would often proceed to redecorate their rooms. This guitarist had a bad drug habit and kept his paraphernalia in the pocket of his guitar case. He left Melbourne, bound for Sydney to catch a connecting flight back to the United States, and in the rush to check out of the Southern Cross had left his guitar behind. When he reached Sydney, the hotel contacted him but he denied that the guitar was his. He was so paranoid about getting busted that he flew home without his $50,000 guitar.

20

'Never surrender till that final dawn,
Never surrender till that dark cloud's
gone'

Glory Road

In 1986, I was still managed by Michael Chugg and remained signed to Mushroom. They approached Neil Young about having me as support act on his six-week Australian tour. They left some of my albums with Neil. He must have been impressed because he agreed to have me as his support, and also insisted that I perform for an hour and play encores if prompted by the audience. Hardly the usual deal for a support act!

Two weeks prior to Neil's arrival in March, my band and I went to a party in Sydney's Double Bay after a gig at Cronulla Leagues. There was a bevy of beautiful girls at the party and there were all kinds of shenanigans going on. I had such a good time I passed out; when I woke up in the morning I found myself in a large bed with a Penthouse Pet. My bass player was over the other side with his own Pet.

My sleeping beauty eventually opened her eyes and began squawking at me.

Thus began my very short-lived relationship with Donna the Penthouse Pet. I couldn't remember what had happened the night before. All I knew was that we'd missed our 11 a.m. flight to the Gold Coast. I didn't see Donna again for a couple of weeks.

Shortly afterwards we joined Neil Young and his band Crazy Horse. I was so excited to be on the tour—Young was a real hero of mine—that I forgot all about Donna the Pet.

Our first night was at the Sydney Entertainment Centre. My band and I were ushered into our dressing room, and then I heard Gudinski and Chugg shouting out my name down the corridor.

I poked my head out the door and Gudinski had a rolled-up newspaper, which he was smacking against his hand, while shouting: 'Ralph, you sex god! All the money in the world couldn't buy publicity like this!'

'What the hell are you talking about?' I asked.

They unfurled a copy of the Melbourne *Truth*. The headline read: 'Rock Star. Penthouse Pet. Love Child.' There was a promo photo of me, with a promo photo of Donna right alongside. Apparently, Donna had been Penthouse Pet of the Year several years running, but her career was in decline. So she launched her own publicity campaign in which she claimed she'd had sex with Julio Iglesias and me, was now pregnant with a child and didn't know who was the father. This was, of course, complete bullshit but it was a hell of a headline. (Neil Young got a copy of it, as he later told me, and had it framed on his studio wall.)

After our set at the Entertainment Centre, we came back to the dressing room and bumped into Donna and a bevy of her Penthouse Pet friends. This just sent the Crazy Horse guys wild.

A true rock'n'roll circus was set in motion. Donna and I continued our relationship for a few weeks but she was a real handful—too much for me.

Neil Young was one of my earliest icons and biggest influences. I took the tour very seriously, at least initially. Neil kept pretty much to himself for the first few gigs, but I hit it off with Crazy Horse from the outset. We partied hard almost every night. It became like one of those legendary tours you only read about in music biographies. There were *Penthouse* and *Playboy* centrefolds hanging around. The partying would go on and on, with only a few hours' sleep between gigs to recharge.

Neil had distanced himself from the rest of us; he obviously didn't need to be around a bunch of hard-living loonies.

When we first played Sydney, Neil stood behind my amplifier for the entire set. He grabbed my arm as I ran off stage, and in view of the cheering audience insisted that I go back out there and play another song. Which I did, of course. Hell, it was Neil Young.

Next time I came off stage he grabbed me again, put his arm around me and said: 'So you're Ralph, huh? You're a bad boy, Ralph. My band hasn't been to bed for two days. I'm gonna change the name of my tour from Rust Never Sleeps to Ralph Never Sleeps!'

He led me down to his dressing room where he had his own private bathroom. Then he took me into the toilet cubicle and locked the door. I assumed that he was going to offer me some drugs, but instead he picked a newspaper off the toilet floor. He was chuckling uncontrollably as he showed me the headline: 'DEAD GIRL ASKS FOR COKE'.

Some young girl was clinically dead for a few minutes, and when the doctors revived her they asked if there was anything she wanted. She asked for a Coca-Cola.

Neil just laughed and laughed, then picked up another newspaper with a headline and accompanying photo of 'flying rabbits'. (It was, of course, a hoax.) Neil told me that Aussies were his favourite bunch of people because we were so weird and wonderful. I couldn't argue with the man.

After the gig that night, I started another party with Crazy Horse members Billy Talbot and Ralph Molina. I asked the guys if they remembered a gig at Wembley Stadium from the seventies. A friend of mine had been at the gig, and told me that Neil was so 'out of it' that his entire on-stage repartee consisted of two comments.

Between songs, Neil slouched over his acoustic guitar and mumbled: 'Go to Miami. Everybody gotta go to Miami. It's cheaper than it looks!'

His only on-stage props were a palm tree in a bucket, a stepladder and a light globe up in the branches of the palm tree. Neil would say: 'Hey, Hal—shine a little sun on me now!'

Then an on-stage extra would mount the ladder, get up into the palm tree branches and twist the light globe to turn the sun on.

Billy and Ralph thought this was an exceptional story, but dismissed it as a rock'n'roll myth. A little later in the evening, Billy asked me what year it might have been.

'I figure that it would have been some time in the mid-seventies.'

'Aw, shit, that's too bad!' Ralph exclaimed. 'In other words, we played to 100,000 people at Wembley Stadium and I don't even remember doin' the gig!'

This wasn't totally out of character. I think the most legendary Neil Young album is *Tonight's the Night*. If you are a big fan, you might recall that this is the set of songs (and the subsequent tour) that Neil and Crazy Horse dedicated to Bruce Berry, their roadie, and Danny Whitten, their guitarist, who'd both died from heroin overdoses.

That night in Sydney, Ralph told me that Neil and some members of the band all lost a year of their minds on a cocktail of drugs and alcohol. The blitz just went on and on. He simply didn't remember the recording sessions, nor did he recall much of the world tour that followed. Maybe they did play Wembley, but he just couldn't remember it.

At the end of the Neil Young tour, Gudinski and I sat in a caravan backstage at a velodrome in Brisbane. I explained to him that I was disenchanted and wanted a release from Mushroom. I was exasperated by how dominant Melbourne was in the overall scheme of Mushroom Records. I also knew that I finally had enough confidence in my own ability to stand alone. Three hours later, the concert well and truly over, the audience gone, Gudinski and I shook hands and parted ways.

The other reason for my disenchantment meant far more to me. I had written a song called 'Goodbye Barbara-Ann' as a tribute to Brian Wilson, celebrating the influence he'd had on all our lives. (Brian Wilson was at his lowest ebb at the time; he was being 'treated' by the mysterious Dr Landy.)

I was over at Triple M one afternoon hanging out and was asked why Mushroom hadn't put more effort into the *Solidarity* album, which barely scraped into the Top 30. The Triple M people felt it was strange, as I had had so much support from radio and the media with the record. Trevor and Jan Smith, who ran the station, asked me if I was still writing songs. I replied that I'd written this song that I was really happy with, but Gudinski had refused to shell out one more cent on my career, so it remained unrecorded.

I played them 'Goodbye Barbara-Ann' and they loved it. I also played it to Charlie Fox, who was the program director. He insisted we play the demo live to air in the drive slot, primetime radio. Among the callers to Triple M that day was a very irate

Gudinski, who abused the shit out of me for daring to play an unreleased track on radio.

Much to Gudinski's further disgust, Sydney radio continued playing the demo. Chuggie stepped in and demanded that Mushroom finance one last single. Gudinski eventually gave us a 'budget' of $2000. This paid for 24 hours' studio time, but musos and people like Chippa, who engineered the session, worked their butts off for free. Unfortunately, the end recording sounded like the dirt-cheap job it was.

I spent much of the mid-1980s living with Jon Farriss and our girlfriends. Jonnie was in a relationship with a Texan gal called Lisa and I'd somehow ended up with Jannike, a Swedish girl with platinum blonde hair and a sexy Scandinavian accent. We'd stay together for a couple of years. For a while, the four of us lived in a smallish flat in Vaucluse, overlooking the ocean. I had been trying to write songs with Jonnie but without much luck.

Things had really started happening for Jon and INXS. They were about to embark on a European club tour to promote the album *Listen Like Thieves*. Just prior to the band's departure from Australia, Gaddafi's terrorists began a campaign of attacks and bombings. We sat there in horror watching the six o'clock news footage of a club in Amsterdam where INXS had been booked to appear—blown to smithereens.

The Farriss brothers went into damage control and stubbornly refused to leave the sanctuary of Australia. Chris Murphy, however, read them the management riot act. The band was going to Europe whether they liked it or not. The girls and I went out to the airport to see off Jonnie and the rest of the band, and were all very concerned for their safety. It was a bloody scary time.

As soon as we arrived back at the flat, I went straight into the studio and wrote the song 'Glory Road' for Jon and INXS and how they fitted into the big world picture during those troubled times. In the song, I depicted them as a group of intrepid Australians off to the front. My lyric described a bunch of dudes trying to climb the mountain of success and bring happiness to a lot of people, at the same time not really understanding why life has to be so complicated. I got a good song out of the experience.

My friend Kerryn Tolhurst, who'd been living in New York, had been stricken with cancer. He had no medical insurance and I helped arrange a benefit concert at Selina's in Sydney. It really was a matter of life and death and I threw myself into a crazy schedule. I only had days to bring together the pick of Australia's rock talent. A few people in the business thought I was mad.

Colleen Ironside, my agent at the Harbour Agency, willingly threw herself into the project. After several sleepless days we managed to form a coalition of Cold Chisel and Midnight Oil, a homegrown supergroup. The press and Triple M promoted the shit out of the gig and we managed to raise something like $40,000 for Kerryn, who over time recovered. This was probably the first benefit concert for a comrade in need, a great tradition that continues today.

Peter Garrett from the Oils called me soon after. He asked me to help promote a gig at Selina's to raise funds so he could have a tilt at the Senate. This time I got really ambitious and organised a cast of thousands, including the Divinyls, Jimmy Barnes, James Reyne, Angry Anderson—who'd be the MC—and, once again, Midnight Oil and Cold Chisel playing together.

Peter Garrett went on holidays in the Whitsunday Passage, leaving me to organise *his* gig. Peter would call me every so often to inquire how it was going. I'd ask him to get back to Sydney and start rehearsing. Rob Hirst and Peter Gifford from the Oils sat out in the beer garden of Selina's, ribbing me that Garrett wouldn't front for his own gig.

I became more and more manic; sleep became a luxury I could ill afford. Rob Hirst kept ribbing me about whether Garrett would even show. I was becoming paranoid. What if he didn't turn up? What would happen then?

The house was full and the show began. Angry came on as MC and things started out really well. But Angry had a stash of bourbon, and as the night progressed, he got more and more sloshed. It was getting out of hand—and Garrett had still not appeared. As I stood in the wings, Angry just lost it. He'd been criticised a lot for his swearing on stage, and had something he felt he needed to say.

'A lotta cunts have bin puttin' shit on me for sayin' "fuck" too much on stage,' Angry roared, as I hid my face in my hands. 'Well, awright, tonight I'm not gonna fuckin' say "fuck" on fuckin' stage and all youse cunts can fuckin' get fucked.'

There were politicians and all manner of toffs in the VIP section. I was freaking out.

There was only one way to solve the problem. I had the only key to a backstage room and recruited Angry's bodyguard—a man known as Fur—to help me get Angry to this room and try to sober him up. The show needed a sober compere. We grabbed Angry and trooped around to my private room. I opened the door. Lo and behold, there was Peter Garrett, watching TV. Angry morphed into this little raging tiger; he pounced on Garrett, screaming that he was a 'bald-headed pseudo intellectual arsehole'—or words to that effect.

Fur grabbed Angry with both arms and held him off the ground, his legs swinging in the air, so he couldn't get to Garrett, who was up on the bed doing some kind of martial arts routine—curiously just like his stage moves. The two Oils roadies were holding Garrett back. I was getting ready for my first heart attack.

A disaster was averted by Fur and the roadies. I calmed Peter down and started working out a strategy for his on-stage entrance. I took him down to the stage, where the Chisel/Oils band was working up a storm, playing 'Shakin' All Over'. The crowd was peaking. There were about ten, maybe eleven microphones along the front of the stage. Peter calmly walked out on stage and the place erupted. He then methodically removed every last mic stand until there was only one remaining, centre stage. Then he launched into his Peter Garrett routine and it was like a musical earthquake. It was definitely one of the most awesome performances I've seen from anyone, anywhere.

I'd been ridiculed by various industry insiders, who said that I'd never pull off the event, but Garrett in full force made all the drama worthwhile.

21

'These are the days we have been
waiting for so long,
But now is the time to set things right'

Distant Thunder

I can't remember the exact circumstances of first meeting Rod Muir—these were crazy hazy days—but I'm pretty sure it was backstage at a Jimmy Barnes gig at the Entertainment Centre. I'd heard the stories about this *enfant terrible*, the legendary alchemist of Australian radio, who had an unbeatable track record. He'd brought in huge changes at 2SM back in the late 1960s, and then led the change to FM radio in the 1980s. Legend has it that when he sold one of his companies, he urged a studio engineer to chainsaw an oak boardroom table in half as the new owners looked on in horror.

Rod was an awe-inspiring character, and without him there wouldn't be contemporary Australian radio as we know it. Because of Rod we musos created one of the twentieth century's greatest subcultures, Oz Rock.

My first impressions of Rod are still indelibly stamped on my brain; I'm pretty sure he had that effect on everyone who met him. Rod was a wild and crazy guy, yet strangely hypnotic. His eyes accurately mirrored what was going on in his head.

He's one of the most extraordinary human beings I have ever met, and I've spent a lot of time with some very remarkable people.

After being introduced, Rod launched into one of his raves about Australia and contemporary culture and the country's dire need for cultural icons rather than just sporting heroes.

'You're the modern day Banjo Paterson,' he said to me. 'I'd like to see a book written about you.'

There I stood, trying my best to be polite and keep up with his bombardment of words—the man spat out a hundred ideas per minute. When Rod was passionate about something, everyone had to keep up or piss off.

Rod became the proud owner of the Triple M network in 1980, and he approached me to co-write songs and produce music in honour of his racing yacht, *Doctor Dan*. (Doctor Dan was the ubiquitous winged guitar-playing satyr from the Triple M logo.) This kickstarted an incredible and sometimes volcanic friendship that endured for some years.

I introduced Rod to Jimmy Barnes, INXS and Jimmy's sister-in-law Jeppy, who'd marry Diesel in 1989. I coined the phrase 'welcome to the party that never ends', because that captured the mood perfectly.

Rod and his wife Kathy lived in a beautiful apartment opposite the yacht club at Darling Point and on Rod's invitation I became part of the furniture. He'd call at any hour; I was spending more time at Rod's house than my own flat. Because of the daily ritual of drinking—French champagne, mostly—it became a very long lost weekend.

What made this different from my wild past was that Rod was well on his way to becoming one of the wealthiest people in Australia; we were living in supreme decadence. Rod had a limousine company on speed dial, cases of Dom Pérignon nearby and a kitchen full of the finest foods from all over the world. If he and Kathy felt like getting away, they would simply phone an airline and book themselves off to Colorado or Tokyo or London or New York, to eat in the world's best restaurants and shop at Harrods or Saks Fifth Avenue. I only caught up on sleep when Rod and Kathy took off overseas.

I took to this fantastic life like a duck to water. Who wouldn't? I began hanging out with Rod's new yachtie mates over at the club, and sailed with the crew on the twilight races around Sydney Harbour. They'd christened Rod 'Mad Max—Beyond Thunderdome'. Rod and I became the definitive odd couple, hanging out together at Benny's.

One night, after another long session there, I crawled home at about 6 a.m. An hour later there was a terrible banging on my front door. I pretended not to hear. The banging increased in intensity; whoever it was, they weren't going away. I peeked out of my bedroom to see a large figure looming at the front door. I thought it might have been a cop and I freaked.

Suddenly Rod's voice came booming through the front door. Still out of it, I struggled down the hall to let him in. He burst inside shouting, 'Where the fuck have you been? Come on, I want you to come into the station.'

The radio station? He had to be kidding.

'Fuck off, Rod, I can't,' I groaned, explaining that I'd only been asleep for an hour.

'I know what'll fix you up, mate,' Rod said, as he grabbed me and pushed me into a cold shower. I poured myself into some clothes, then we jumped into his Mercedes coupé and sped off to Bondi Junction.

Rod had invited Jack Mundey, the trade union leader and left-wing activist, to lunch in the Triple M boardroom. Rod had his own chef and waiter on call; I now knew them both quite well. By the time Jack arrived, I really wasn't hungry, but was directed to my place at the table. Jack became increasingly agitated that Rod had white linen and sterling silver cutlery and a waiter in a tuxedo serving several courses of food.

'Why the fuck do we have to have three forks, Rod?' he shouted.

'Well, one's for the entree, one for main course and one for dessert.'

'What a fucking crock of shit!' Mundey thundered across the table. 'Two-thirds of the world are starving to death and can't even afford one knife and fork. Waiter, take these away!'

Rod and I also surrendered two of our forks. Then Jack began ranting and raving about the waiter being a slave to the *petite bourgeoisie* (that'd be Rod and me, in Jack's eyes). Jack suddenly sprang to his feet, swapped clothes with the waiter, demanded that the waiter be seated—and Jack began serving our lunch. Much to Jack's dismay, I had to let him know that the waiter actually had several jobs, and had two boys attending a very elite Sydney boarding school.

NSW Premier Nick Greiner came up to the station one day, seeking Rod's advice about how he could best capture the 'youth vote' at the forthcoming elections. Rod and I were both having a grand old time—I could barely conceal my mirth—when Rod grabbed Greiner by the arm and hauled him into the boardroom. He cued up AC/DC's 'Highway to Hell' at painful volume. The premier sat there, his ears pinned back against the boardroom wall, trying to look cool. It was just too much for me. When the track finished, Rod started shouting, 'Capture the youth vote, Nick? Capture the youth vote? That's how you're gonna capture the youth vote, Nick—and you'd better bloody believe it!'

These were extraordinary times. Rod and Kathy and I partied almost every day yet we did regular newspaper, TV and radio interviews—I always seemed to be involved with something or other on Triple M. The scariest thing Rod ever made me do was deliver a speech to all of Triple M's sponsors. Now, I can sing in front of two million people (as I did one New Year's Eve on national television), and I bluff my way through TV interviews, but I'm totally unaccustomed to public speaking. I just stood on this podium, speechless and petrified, but the sponsors gave me a hearty round of applause anyway.

'What are you all clapping for?' I shouted. 'I haven't even said anything.'

More cheers and applause.

I have no regrets about my years with this whirling dervish called Rod Muir; he really taught me all about pushing the envelope. To him, sleeping was a waste of time—and watching TV was a complete waste of life, reserved for losers and no hopers. I was also hanging out with INXS and Jimmy Barnes constantly, along with our entourage of hedonists and crazies. It was really quite a circus.

Chuggie, who was also a good friend of Rod's, called me in 1985 to say that Rod wanted the band and me up on Hamilton Island, to play on the final night of the yacht races around the Whitsundays. I was dumbfounded; this was going to cost $15,000 to $20,000. Chuggie shouted me down.

'Just get things organised, Ralph,' he told me.

He told me that Rod would pay all my expenses on Hamilton Island for a week or so. I just wasn't used to anyone having so much money on tap.

I was flown up to the island first class and put up in one of the very pleasant bures. On my first day, I was out on a rented Hobie Cat with Rod, racing against Warwick Rooklyn, a rich mate of his. A very strong wind blew up and we all started getting a bit silly. To my shock, Rod headed straight for the other boat. I assumed he would change tack before we rammed them. No such luck. Welcome to Rod's world! We rammed Warwick's boat so hard that we actually speared through its deck. Both boats were virtually written off. Warwick and Rod both thought this was the funniest thing ever.

We pulled ourselves out of the water and Rod and Warwick immediately offered to pay for both catamarans—just like that. Problem solved.

The Whitsundays are decadent enough when occupied by regular people on holiday, but when a few hundred yachties with their respective barbarian millionaire patrons take over, beware. The sun was sweltering one day and Rod ordered us all into the pool. He then ordered a bucket full of Mai Tais—at $600 a bucket. Crazy times.

Rod and Keith Williams, the lord of Hamilton Island, had a nasty falling out about Rod organising the concert with my band and me. Keith just didn't like the idea. Yet again, no problem. Rod organised for a sand barge to be dragged from Airlie Beach on the mainland, complete with a substantial sound system.

The night was incredible, one of the biggest ever on the island. Several hundred wasted yachties looked on as an equally trashed band played for almost five hours. Rod's impressive boat *Doctor Dan* was moored behind the floating stage; we used it as a dressing room. I was told that at various points of the evening I'd stumble off stage and would be found on the boat, hiding down below with Rod.

My drummer was a guy named John Lee, who was originally from the Dingoes. The high point of the evening was John doing a big drum roll at the end of 'I Am an Island' and diving straight into the ocean. He then staggered up to my microphone and shouted: 'Aw shit! I just realised you've all been pissing in the water, you scumbags!'

We were still playing when the sun came up, and wound down from the gig with breakfast. We all staggered into the restaurant and I ordered a pitcher of Bloody Marys to go with our Weet-Bix. By now, the epic party was definitely on its last legs. Then I noticed wild flames in the kitchen; I realised that all the restaurant staff were also out of their brains and could barely function.

One kitchen hand shouted to his mate: 'Fire? What do we do?'

'Fucked if I know,' said his fellow kitchen hand.

The staff had no fire extinguishers. This was unbelievable. A few minutes later and the fire was raging out of control. A hopelessly wasted Harvey James was standing on the side of the dolphins' pool, trying to figure out how he was going to save the poor beasts. The rest of us did our best to save Harvey.

Within 15 or 20 minutes, the fire destroyed the central portion of the resort. Some end to some party.

❖

The following year, 1986, with much of the resort rebuilt, Rod decided to risk staging the concert again. This time I formed a band with Jon Farriss on drums, Garry Gary Beers on bass, Ian Moss on guitar and Murray Burns from the band Mi-Sex on keyboards. Rod was right in the middle of being profiled by *60 Minutes*—the crew followed him up to Hamilton Island—so I had Rod and George Negus on backing vocals. Quite a band.

Jon and I arrived with our respective girlfriends several days early, as did Garry Gary, and Michael Long, their tour manager. As soon as we checked in, the new staff was very curt; they warned us that if there was any more trouble, we'd be thrown off the island. Jonnie and I were flabbergasted.

During the first couple of days we were singled out and the staff blatantly discriminated against us. They wouldn't rent us catamarans or golf buggies and were rude and unreasonable. Apologetic staff later told us that Dire Straits had occupied the island for an extended 'end of tour' party and had gone berserk and trashed the place. So we were tarred with the same brush!

The second gig proved to be just as outrageous as the first. Once again we played for about five hours and the band and audience were wasted, absolutely wrecked. At one point I disappeared off stage and left Mossy up there singing lead vocals on 'I Shot the Sheriff'. Mossy started berating me over the PA; he couldn't remember the words so he kept singing the chorus over and over again. We just managed to get to bed before the sun came up—and this time the resort didn't burn down.

22

'The Underground
it doesn't matter if it's night or day'

The Underground

I received a phone call from Rod's secretary; Rod was competing in a yacht race and had summoned me to LA. I protested that this was really going too far (literally) and that I didn't have a passport or US visa—nor did I have any money. I was mixing with some wealthy people, but I was broker than I'd ever been. But there was no denying Rod Muir. All the documentation was promptly arranged and within a couple of days I was winging my way to Los Angeles.

Rod, Kathy, Eric Robinson and Chuggie were all at LAX to meet me and I was whisked away to the Marina del Rey Hotel. At the bar they broke the news to me that I was sharing a room with Chuggie. The yacht crew was busy most days, so Chuggie and I entertained ourselves. He was still basically my manager, although the lines between business and pleasure had become blurred. Jimmy Barnes was in town recording; his wife Jane was with him, so I spent a lot of time up in Beverly Hills with the Barneses. We were actually quite well behaved—for a change—and I'd usually return to Marina del Rey well before midnight, ready for an early morning wake-up.

One night I got into a taxi with a huge black cab driver. I had about $US30 on me and watched the meter shoot up to $40 and beyond. I was concerned; I knew LA well enough to know you could get murdered for less.

As soon as we pulled up at the door of the hotel, I made the excuse that I'd have to go inside and get the extra $20 from my manager. I rushed into the room and Chuggie was drunk, arguing over the phone with his fiancée in Australia. An empty bottle of cognac was on the table, his mood was ugly.

'I need some money, Chuggie,' I said.

He refused. I went back to the taxi and nervously tried to explain the situation to the driver. I feared for my life.

'Look,' I said, 'I don't have the money. My manager won't give me any.'

To my surprise, he threw his head back and laughed. He told me that he'd once been a very successful musician and that Chuggie's behaviour didn't surprise him at all. He insisted that we forget about it and wished me all the best with my career.

Another lucky escape.

I came back to the room, and Chuggie and I got into the biggest fight.

I stormed out of the room, up to the reception desk and demanded that the hotel get me as far away from my ex-manager as possible. The receptionist told me he'd also been an entertainer—this was LA, after all—and found my situation very familiar. He moved me into a smart new room. Fortunately, by now the 22-man yachtie entourage was about ready to set sail for Honolulu, competing in what was known as the Transpac Race.

Chuggie and I didn't speak for days. When Rod and his crew set sail on *Doctor Dan*, Chuggie and I flew to Hawaii. We boarded a flight packed with holidaying families—it was delayed for five hours. We got so drunk on board we raised hell all the way, shouting and laughing at a lousy Dudley Moore movie.

In Waikiki we checked into a hotel. For the next couple of days I was constantly harangued by street dealers, trying to sell me various drugs. I guess I looked like the archetypal rock muso, with my shades and jeans and T-shirt.

It seemed I couldn't walk 10 metres without hearing the call: 'Hey, man, you wanna score? What do you say, brother?'

I either ignored them or shut them down if they persisted.

Chuggie's bad mood continued. He simply didn't want to be there. On the Saturday night we went out for dinner at a Japanese restaurant right in Waikiki. Chugg got stuck into the cognac and demanded that I put the bill on my delinquent credit card.

He then apologised for his grumpy mood and explained that someone had promised that he would score him some great pot in California but hadn't come through. Without something to smoke, Chuggie just wasn't himself.

'Why didn't you tell me?' I asked.

I told him how I'd been pestered by drug dealers for the last couple of days. Waikiki on a Saturday night is much like Kings Cross at peak hour, and there we were, standing at a pedestrian crossing, when Chuggie shouted: 'I want some fuckin' drugs!' at the top of his voice. I freaked. I couldn't believe he could be this irresponsible.

A young black kid on a skateboard swerved up to us. He told us he had the best 'heads' in Hawaii; we could score for $175. He kept his gaze set on me, while looking suspiciously at Chuggie—perhaps he thought he was a cop. I explained that I was a rock musician from Australia and Chuggie was my manager. The kid seemed satisfied, though still a little nervous.

We agreed to the deal and the kid returned a few minutes later with a rolled-up *Rolling Stone* tucked under his arm. We strolled into a quiet arcade and Chuggie pulled a wad of cash from his pocket. He was thumbing through the notes and counting out the first 20 dollars.

Chuggie paid out the full $175 and we made off back to the car park. On the drive back to the hotel, Chuggie rolled a huge 'Bob Marley' joint—a four-paper number—and began smoking it in the car. From the corner of my eye I noticed that it was having no effect on him whatsoever. When we pulled up to the front door of the hotel, I bade Chuggie goodnight and tried to escape from the car. He held me by the arm and gave me a menacing look. He'd just bought an ounce of compressed oregano leaf; I didn't know whether to laugh or cry.

I had to get back home to Australia. This trip was turning into a nightmare. I had fulfilled my obligation to Rod, which was essentially to promote the song he and I had written called 'The Transpac Slide'. I did a couple of radio interviews and we tried to set up an American release for the record but without success.

As I packed my bags, I discovered that my passport was missing. Shit. Because it was a weekend there was no chance of me replacing it, so I kicked up such a drama that Rod's secretary made special arrangements for me with the Department of Foreign Affairs office back in Canberra, and I boarded a flight to Australia without a passport. Rod certainly was well connected.

All the way back to Australia, I noticed a crumpled figure hiding underneath a stack of clothing, stretched out across a row of seats in economy. When we finally reached Sydney, the dishevelled character turned out to be John Woodruff. 'Woody' was the manager of Icehouse, Diesel and the Angels (and later on, Savage Garden).

'You've got buckley's of getting back in the country without a passport,' Woody said to me.

I told him that all the customs officers at Sydney airport were big fans of mine who'd given me the VIP treatment the last few times I'd re-entered Australia. These customs officers would stand around and make very loud jokes about me importing drugs and all kinds of contraband in the correct manner.

'Richard, did ya hide it in the lining properly, like we told ya last time?' they'd ask me.

'Yes,' I'd reply sheepishly, then they'd whisk me through the side door, much to the envy and exasperation of my fellow passengers.

This occasion was no different. The immigration officers sought me out from the giant queue of passengers. I had just enough time to wave to Woodruff before I was escorted out the same side door.

I'd broken up with Jannike, and knew it was time to pull back from the edge, at least for a little while. Hedonism and self-indulgence can be fun, but it can also turn boring and repetitive. Perhaps embracing life's Yin and Yang is the most essential way for a creative person to live. If I stayed straight and boring all the time my work lacked soul. On the other hand, if I lived in a world of inebriated chaos, my work wouldn't make any sense.

I'd had my latest period of chaos, now it was time to sit down and apply myself in a clear and sober light. Accordingly, I started writing songs for what was to become the *Glory Road* album. They were equal parts inspiration and perspiration. And making the record would take me to some amazing places.

After the end of my time with Mushroom Records, I'd been unable to land a new record deal. I'd also been preoccupied playing around with Rod and Kathy, INXS and the extended Barnes family, including Jep Mahoney. Jep, Jon Farriss and I became the three musketeers for a while. We hung out together constantly.

Anyway, one night Jon and Jimmy took it upon themselves to suggest to Rod Muir that he finance an album for me—in exchange, they'd guarantee the record was given the best possible support. Rod, typically, embraced the idea with gusto and set in motion what were perhaps the most fascinating and adventurous recording sessions for any Australian album.

By now, I'd written several songs, and recorded one ('Angelou') with the patronage of 'Chippa' Nicholas, in an unsuccessful stab at an independent production.

INXS were in hiatus and Jon wanted to work with me on this new project; he badly needed a bit of respite, to step away from the madness of INXS for a while. Without much ado, and now with Rod's backing, we engaged Mark Opitz to produce the album, booked time at Sydney's EMI studios and got to work. Chippa was engineering, Jon played drums, Garry Gary Beers was on bass and Alan Mansfield played keyboards.

We soon realised however, that Mark's mind was simply not on the job. So it became apparent that this was simply not going to work. Finally, after a couple of days, Mark decided to leave my album and move on to another project, and this ended up being the best decision all round for him and for us.

We were liberated overnight, and started having a ball in the studio. We had some amazing jam sessions; Jon and Garry Gary were able to really stretch out and put in some fantastic performances. Select friends would come in and hang out and we would play on into the wee small hours. We all found it so easy to be creative, writing songs together and then recording them while they were fresh.

Jon and Garry Gary started jamming on a reggae feel and I pulled it into some shape—it became 'The Underground'. I'm pretty sure we wrote and recorded that in one night.

We recorded most of the initial stuff for *Glory Road* very professionally and didn't really get up to much mischief. In the first couple of weeks Jeppy was the only visitor—and she was like 'family' anyway. It was a very tight unit. Then we shifted camp to Rhinoceros Studios in Darlinghurst and the whole nature of the project took a turn for the surreal.

As the months of 1987 rolled by, my family unit of Rod and Kathy, Jim and Jane, Jeppy and INXS grew substantially, as we played host to much of the Sydney music industry. In the studio with us were Marc Hunter, Alan Mansfield and other members of Dragon, plus Sharon O'Neill, along with industry people like Mark Pope and Richard McDonald. The clientele of Benny's crashed their way in most nights. The same team of INXS and Chippa had by now started work on the *Kick* album and there wasn't much delineation between the two projects.

Jonnie and I were now sharing a flat that he and the other INXS guys owned in Kirribilli and we started to live like vampires; the days seemed to seamlessly meld into nights in the studio that never ended. We just came home to sleep.

One night Jon was having a very intense session with Alan Mansfield, trying to coax an almost impossible keyboard part out of him, while Sharon O'Neill and I sat in the anechoic chamber writing bizarre lyrics and sculling a bottle of Scotch, working on a song, 'Under the Knife', which, if it was ever recorded, would have featured one of the most bizarre and chilling lyrics of all time. It captured the mood perfectly.

Soon after, Michael Hutchence and an entourage of his strange friends burst into the studio, all tripping on acid. Michael was wearing a crushed velvet purple cape; he was flying around the room like a 1968 hippie throwback. Michael wouldn't stop—the lunacy went on for hours.

When Michael and his 'acid' friends left us, they went back to Hutch's suite at the Park Hyatt, Sydney's best hotel. The party rolled on, all the way to the hotel's roof. Somehow they got up there with a 'ghetto blaster' and continued the party.

THE UNDERGROUND

Fortunately, the Park Hyatt staff was used to INXS's hijinks. On another night, I was partying with Jon when Kirk summoned me down to Michael's suite. It must have been 5 a.m. Kirk had the key so we let ourselves in. What I saw was quite a sight. There was Hutch, spreadeagled in the ensuite, with two women straddling him and giggling hysterically. They were all in their underwear.

'Hey, Rikki,' someone called out. 'Come and play ride 'em horsies with us, man!'

If that wasn't enough, this was the same night I returned to Jonnie's room and there was a crazed Gary Busey, the American actor, hammering on the door, threatening to kill us if we didn't shut up. Madness.

23

'There's just one thing we don't understand,
Whatever happened to the emperor's pants'

Emperor's New Clothes

Halfway through the recording of *Glory Road*, Jon organised a session with Michael Hutchence, Tim Farriss and Garry Gary Beers; together we'd all co-write a song for the album. While I was on the phone in the control room, I could hear INXS jamming on one of their biggest hits. They kept playing it over and over so finally I went in and asked what they were doing.

'We're writing your song, Richie!'

I said they should stop bullshitting around.

'When are you going to get serious about this?' I asked. It turns out they were serious; they were writing the music 'bed' for the co-write, using their own song as the starting point.

I didn't know what to say.

Tim gave me a hug.

The sun went down and we started partying and I threw all caution to the wind. I settled in with Hutch to write the lyric. This was a big deal for me, a real privilege, because I've always regarded Michael as one of the great rock lyricists of our time.

EMPEROR'S NEW CLOTHES

This was the day in October 1986 that former PM Malcolm Fraser woke up in a seedy Memphis hotel without his pants and passport, with no idea what had happened to him. Perfect fodder for a rock lyric.

We whacked it down as a band with Michael and me adjusting the lyrics as we went along, and ended up with the 'Emperor's New Clothes'. Jimmy Barnes turned up later that night and he and Hutch did a spectacular backing vocal part; their ad-libs on the outro of the track were perfect.

When there was no time available at Rhinoceros, we moved to Paradise Studios, the other great studio in town. It was here that Jimmy recorded the backing vocals for the song 'Trust Somebody'. The control room at Paradise was so small it was claustrophobic; Jimmy stood centimetres away from Chippa and me while attempting to sing unbelievably high vocal parts.

Chippa sheepishly offered to 'varispeed'—that is, slow the tape down, so as to lower the pitch of the recording and make it more plausible for Jimmy to sing. He'd have none of it. Jimmy would go into this frightening martial arts routine, involving lots of screaming and primal grunts, then he'd yell: 'NOW ROLL IT!'

Much to our disbelief, after many hours, Jimmy recorded vocals so high and beyond his normal range that even Ian Moss, his bandmate, believed it was a woman singing.

Jimmy convinced Rod Muir that I needed a Gibson 335 guitar to record my parts on 'Trust Somebody'. It was about

5 p.m. and the studio was a few kilometres from Venue Music, the main music store in the city. Rod and I jumped in his limo and went screaming down to Venue. I asked whether I could borrow a 335 for a day or two so I could record my parts and as contra give Venue a credit on the album. They immediately agreed.

However, Rod asked about the price of the guitar. It was $5000. Despite my protestations, Rod bought the guitar for me on the spot. What a gesture.

❖

I asked Ian Moss to come and play some guitar on the album. This was Jonnie's first gig as producer, and he was now playing the role of headmaster, as I'd done with INXS during *Underneath the Colours*. He booked Ian for a midday start, but Mossy turned up a few hours late, so things got a little uncomfortable. I recommended that Jon go home and I'd produce Mossy's guitar parts myself.

So we put the track 'Glory Road' up on the tape machine and Mossy settled into the studio. However, Mossy just couldn't seem to get a vibe, and stood out in the studio for ages not playing a single note. Eventually, I went out and spoke with him.

'What's up, Mossy?'

'I just can't get a vibe happening,' he replied, a bit downcast.

I suggested he go upstairs to the recreation room and play pinball for a while. I'd lay down a 'guide guitar' part, which might get him inspired.

I took my brand new 335 out into the studio, and fairly easily recorded a guide solo for Ian to play with. When he came back down to the studio, he still faltered when the tape started rolling. I went out to the studio to see if there was anything else I could do, but he insisted that he liked what I'd played. Big raps from a genuine guitar legend.

'Let's just use that,' Mossy insisted.

However, I persevered and after a while we got a bit of guitar playing out of him. But Ian was right all along. When the album was mixed a few months later, by none other than Chris Lord-Alge, who'd worked with Prince, the Rolling Stones and Madonna, he elected to go with my solo. However, Ian's playing featured everywhere else on the song.

INXS's producer, Englishman Chris Thomas, needed to move the *Kick* album to Paris, because he was due to commence recording in Europe with Paul McCartney. Funnily enough, when INXS were in Rhinoceros, hard at work, a call came in from 'some Pommie bloke called Paul'. He was told to piss off, the band was busy. Guess which Paul that was?

Anyway, Jon Farriss thought it only logical, as the producer of *Glory Road*—and given that most of INXS were playing on my album—that I should relocate to Paris, too. Much to my amazement, Rod agreed. Typically, he took it even further.

So I packed my bags and guitars and flew out to Paris, where I stayed in St James Albany, an eighteenth-century hotel on Rue de Rivoli, opposite the Tuilerie Gardens. This was my home for almost two months, one of the most fantastic times of my life.

We got straight to work at Studios de la Grande Armée, which was in the heart of Paris. The festivities began pretty much from the first night. I started final vocals and threw myself into it, because I was very conscious of what this was costing. (Don't ask.) At first, it was just Jon, Chippa and Philipe la Font, the French assistant engineer, who we christened Fifi la Font. For the first couple of nights we were hard-working professionals.

Then Hutch arrived from Hong Kong. I was out in the studio recording vocals, concentrating on 'Angelou', because Hutch had agreed to sing backing vocals on that track. (Marc Hunter had recorded one backing vocal back in Sydney, leaving the other part free for Michael.)

From my position in the studio, I could sense that the boys in the control room were up to something. When I finally came in about an hour later, I noticed that everyone was on some kind of drug. It turned out that Hutch had brought in a large stash of Halcion tablets from Hong Kong, and had persuaded all the other guys to drop a couple of tabs.

The result was that everyone, except me, lapsed into this warm and fuzzy mood, which had the reverse effect on me—I was pretty bloody irritable. I was really aware of how much money this was costing Rod, and got shitty.

Michael started treating me like a baby, tickling my tummy and saying: 'C'mon, Ricky. It's just like having a joint!'

I had the shits for the rest of the night, but fortunately, finally, Hutch went into the studio and recorded some stellar vocals.

Then Michael turned his attention to Fifi, demanding that he find some coke. Fifi's English was terrible; he couldn't understand a word Michael was saying. Finally Michael just bellowed in exasperated pseudo French: 'Cooooo-caaaaine!'

'Oh, *oui*,' said Fifi. 'You should have said. The Stones used this studio last month, and I think Keith and Ronnie probably dropped many, many grams of residue down into the console.'

Now, a Neve console is made up of twenty-four removable modules, which can be easily unscrewed by hand. While the rest of us were trying to work, Fifi and Michael began unscrewing some of the modules. After they'd removed about half a dozen, we, the workers, loudly protested that they were disrupting the session—there was a gaping hole in the recording console.

Fifi made a phone call to a dealer who promptly delivered a number of grams. I had a new manager, a guy named Gary

Grant, and when he arrived at the studio the whole evening became a big, blurry get-together. I surrendered and we all went back to St James Albany to party.

We congregated in Chippa's room, joined by some of the girls in our entourage. It all started out reasonably well, joints were being passed around, along with some booze and a few lines. Then the Halcion thing started to veer out of control. Michael was handing them out like lollies; I went from party pooper to the life of the damned party in a heartbeat. As many of you will know, the barbiturate family of drugs really mess with your head; they erase your memory and generally make a real mess of you. So don't ask me what happened that night. I just don't know.

But I have been given first-hand reports. Apparently, I attempted to make it back to my room, but the hallways of St James Albany have little sets of stairs, six steps at regular intervals throughout the hotel. I just didn't make it to my room.

I was found comatose, in a foetal position, on one of those little flights of stairs. A few hotel staff carefully and gently carried me back to my room and put me to bed.

This became a running joke. For the remainder of my stay, every time I'd drift in from the studio at around 2 a.m., the reception staff would smile.

'*Bonsoir*, Rikki—would you like us to tucky-tuck you into bed, or will you be all right tonight?'

Titter titter, giggle giggle. Hardy bloody ha ha.

As I lay dozing on the stairwell, the rest of the entourage decided to walk to a friend's apartment and continue the party there. I don't know how they did it; I certainly wouldn't have been able to manage it. When they opened the door, Chippa was so maggoted he bounced off all four walls and fell backwards onto a glass coffee table. Being drunk, he didn't hurt himself, but it made a hell of a commotion, especially at 5 a.m.

The little old lady who lived in the apartment downstairs called the gendarmes. Michael and Gary, meanwhile, had retired to a bedroom with a couple of the girls, and had just gotten naked when the cops arrived. The cops handcuffed Gary to a chair in the middle of the room. Hutch then strolled out of the bedroom, naked, an unlit cigarette hanging out of his mouth.

'Got a light, Gaz?' he asked.

'No, fuckhead. As you can see, the police have arrived and I'm naked and handcuffed to a chair!'

'Oh. No need to snap,' exclaimed Hutch in his inimitably cool style.

Now, remember I was sleeping like a baby and I promise you I was nowhere near the apartment. I hereby proclaim my innocence.

So imagine my shock when my girlfriend back in Sydney opened her morning paper to read: 'MICHAEL HUTCHENCE AND RICHARD CLAPTON ARRESTED IN PARIS. NAKED AND HANDCUFFED TO CHAIR.' She promptly called me and gave me my notice.

Triple M had a field day with the story, treating us like heroes, as did most of Australia. Only trouble was this: I wasn't even there. I raged and ranted at my manager Gary for setting me up like that. He calmly qualified his actions—for it was he who had sent out the press release—by pointing out that some bloke called Gary was unknown to the general populace and was of no interest. But I had a name and albums to sell; this was just par for the course. Hype! It was far from funny, although I can laugh about it now.

We actually adopted a serious work ethic after the first couple of nights' shenanigans. We turned up to work at Studios de la Grande Armée each morning at 10 and worked solidly until midnight, and the partying became less frequent. Every morning Chippa and I would recoil at the sight of Fifi La Font tucking into his steak tartare; I can't think of anything worse for breakfast than a slab of raw steak with a raw egg dumped on top. Life in the studio was relatively sane.

However, on the night of my birthday, we booked ourselves a very long table at La Coupole (Ernest Hemingway's favourite brasserie). There were maybe a dozen of us there, but no Michael Hutchence. He'd been partying in the South of France most of the week.

However, after a while Hutch appeared, looking the worse for wear. He made a beeline for me and plonked himself down in my lap.

He let out a yelp. 'Rikki! I haven't been to bed for three days, and boy, do I need a line!'

'Shit, Michael,' I answered, 'don't look at me!'

I seem to recall my last sight of Michael was of him disappearing in the direction of the men's room.

The next time I caught up with Hutch, we were mucking about in someone's room and he threw a chair out the window—from four floors up. Chippa told me that the hotel charged him $1200 for damages—seventeenth-century furniture doesn't come cheap.

Richard Lowenstein, the Melbourne filmmaker who'd been responsible for most of INXS's clips, arrived in Paris to start filming a video for my 'Glory Road' single. We'd be shooting in Paris and East and West Berlin. We started with a couple of days filming in the Tuilerie Gardens, just across the road from our hotel.

Jon, his Texan girlfriend Lisa and I rented a car and drove to Berlin for stage two of the shoot. We were looking sartorially splendid, all decked out in Yohji Yamamoto linen outfits. I'd banged on about the wonders of Berlin to Jonnie for so many years that it was a very personal, special adventure.

I took Jon and Lisa to all my old haunts and we spent a few really special days driving out to Wannsee, where I'd written most of *Prussian Blue*, and Klausenerplatz and Schloss Charlottenburg, where I had first lived in the commune.

I introduced Jon and Lisa to Volker and Andrea and we had a hilarious night in all the best bars in Berlin. Lisa ended up getting very drunk, and started to irritate a few of the Berlin University crowd, who were Volker's colleagues. She demanded—in her strong Texan accent—that the Germans teach her how to say 'Get fucked' so she could tell them all to get fucked in their native dialect. A sort of cultural exchange.

Unfortunately, she just couldn't get her tongue around it, so she did the rounds of the entire bar, telling them all—or so she thought—to get fucked. The Germans were egging her on, making strange little birdy noises and howling with laughter. The more they laughed the more outraged she became. The Germans were laughing louder and louder, because she was telling them to *get finched*—you know, like a finch, the little birdy! Too much vodka will do that to you.

Jon and Lisa were staying at the Kempinski, a wonderful old world Berlin hotel with an illustrious history. Jeppy had arrived and was also staying there. I was holed up in Volker's apartment. Gary Grant had flown to New York, where Chris Lord-Alge was mixing my album. Chris had laid down the law—he insisted that Jon and I could not be present at the mix.

A very strange series of events took place one night at the Kempinski. The four of us had been out to dinner, and were in a very jovial mood. When we arrived back at the hotel there were a number of messages for me from Gary in New York urging me to call him immediately at the studio, but he also gave strict instructions that Jon wasn't to know about the phone call.

I wrote the NY number on a notepad in Jon's room and then went around to Jeppy's room alone to make the call. But Jonnie, who suspected something was up, was no fool. Like a true Cold War spy, Jonnie used a pencil to lift the impression of the New York number off his notepad, just like in the movies. Before I even got to Jeppy's room, Jonnie had phoned Chris and a full-scale argument broke out.

Chris, apparently, didn't like certain aspects of Jon's production work and had wanted my approval to change a few things. Jon and Chris were at loggerheads; Chris dug in and refused to listen to Jon's point of view. When I arrived back in Jonnie's room, they were still yelling at each other. It had degenerated into a battle of egos.

Needless to say, at the listening party at the legendary Air Studios in London, a couple of weeks later, everybody gave Lord-Alge's mixes the thumbs up. That is the record you've been hearing all these years. And what a record: Sydney, Paris, Berlin, London, Amsterdam, back and forth, back and forth. Quite a journey.

24

'music soothes the savage beast
let's go up where the angels fly'

Up Where The Angels Fly

We drove back to Amsterdam, arrived about midnight, checked into the American Hotel and went looking for coffee. We found a place that looked innocent enough, and Jon insisted that I try the cake.

'It's the best cake in the world, you know,' he told me.

Indeed it was delicious, so I ordered a second slice. Shortly after, I started to complain that I was feeling ill and would have to go back to the hotel. Jon was at first quite concerned, but then quickly realised that I had been eating 'Space Cake', loaded with hashish. I wasn't sick, I was stoned out of my brain.

Back at the American, still in our fabulously expensive linen Yohji outfits, Jon and I reclined together in a bath full of water and floating Heineken bottles, which bobbed around us in the tub.

Richard Lowenstein had hired twenty-two people for the shoot. I nearly fell over when I saw them all the next morning. He had a full German film crew, a producer from Ireland who had worked on most of U2's videos, a catering crew, and his personal assistant Troy, from Melbourne, who, according to legend, had worked as a female shop assistant at David Jones in Melbourne for many years. They also recruited four German girls from a nightclub to mime the backing vocals, no doubt promising to make them stars when they were seen all over the world.

The first day's shoot in West Berlin went off without a hitch; it was an excellent day's work. We were then to move to East Berlin, where I'd had my share of unpleasant and sometimes scary experiences in the past, so you could understand my trepidation. As we crossed Checkpoint Charlie, smuggling in professional film cameras and all sorts of equipment, I'd convinced myself that if we did end up in an East German prison or, worse still, Siberia, then it'd be a glorious way to go out. It was all art for art's sake, anyway.

However, luckily we got through without a hitch. There was a huge entertainment complex—if you could call it that—named The People's Palace, right in the centre of East Berlin. Once we'd converted our currency into East German marks, it became useless, so one had to spend it all before leaving the DDR.

So off we went to The People's Palace and got rotten on Russian vodka for about ten cents a shot, drinking until we'd run out of East German marks. I became a little nervous when my party started to shout and laugh and generally carry on in a very rowdy fashion. I was understandably nervous about attempting to cross back into West Berlin.

By this time, Troy had started to yell and whistle and behave in a very camp manner. He insisted on being the first of our party to enter the private booths where the East German Police interrogated everyone individually.

Once inside a booth, Troy began giggling about how cute the border cop was, what a nice arse he had, and the rest of it. Believe it or not, we got through okay. Somehow the 'Glory Road' video got made and you can still see it on YouTube today. Three years later the Wall came down.

I returned to Berlin to stay with Volker and his new wife Andrea. Jimmy Barnes had been calling, asking me to fly across to San Francisco where he was hard at work on the *Freight Train Heart* album. He said that if I made the trip, I could get involved in the lyric writing for his album, which he was recording with the American band Journey. It was tempting. I was in a holding pattern, anyway, because there'd be a period of time before WEA would get started with marketing and promo for my *Glory Road* album. I gladly took up Jimmy's offer.

Jimmy called from San Francisco the night before I flew out to make sure I was going to show up.

When I arrived at The Record Plant in Sausalito someone passed a joint around but Jimmy warned: 'I know you, Ralph—don't make a pig of yourself!'

'Of course not,' I replied.

However, Jimmy and Journey were all hard at work and I started to get bored hanging around this big empty recording studio in the middle of the night. I started dabbling—sneaking in a toke here and there until I was really quite stoned.

Jimmy appeared out of nowhere; it felt like an ambush. He was with Randy Jackson, the famous bass player (more recently seen in *American Idol*), who was—and is—super straight. Jimmy was raving about how great my *Glory Road* album was, and then suggested that Randy and I find an empty studio, so he could listen to my LP for himself. So I had to sit in an empty studio, with this squeaky-clean music icon and feign sobriety for over an hour. I could barely talk.

Jim and Jane had rented an enormous house over in Mill Valley, so I moved in. Jimmy's kids, Mahalia and EJ, were very young, so our time at Mill Valley was very civilised, very family friendly.

There was trouble in the studio, however. Journey called an emergency band meeting with Jimmy and laid down the law. They'd written the music for Jimmy's album, and they sure as hell were not going to allow a rank outsider—that would be me—to come in and write all the lyrics. I'd flown all that way for nothing. There was no point trying to fight it, so I decided to treat the San Francisco leg of my journey as a holiday. You could pick worse places.

Things heated up on my return to Australia. I was thrown straight into a whirlwind of work to prepare *Glory Road* for release. Now single again—I'd lost Jannike in the aftermath of the 'naked and handcuffed to a chair' episode with Hutch—I moved into a new place with Jonnie. INXS were now at their worldwide peak, and it was a very exciting time for the band, and equally exciting being around them.

But their success didn't rub off on me. Triple M were the Number One radio station in Australia, and very supportive of *Glory Road*, but there was sniping from some quarters about Rod being my patron while also owning the Austereo network, and we were perhaps overly sensitive to what the public perception of all this might be. I think Rod actually tried to dissuade his staff from pushing the album in any way that could be construed as over the top.

Some idiotic journalist wrote a full-page story in the *Sydney Morning Herald* claiming that *Glory Road* had cost $750,000 and was simply an exercise in hedonism and decadence, to the detriment of the music. This was plain wrong. As with all my other albums, the project was 90 per cent hard work and professionalism, and 10 per cent partying. Sure, in this book I shine a light on the funny and/or interesting stories, because it's a hell of a lot more entertaining than describing the long hours spent getting drum sounds, or how we hauled guitar amps all over the studio in search of the perfect sound, or the fine-tuning involved in mixing an album.

And for the record, *Glory Road* cost $210,000 to make, an average album budget for 1987.

❖

One night, 'Stumpy', my roadie of many years, and I walked into Benny's Bar to find a woman named Susie and a friend of hers cavorting drunkenly up on the bar to the strains of 'My Way'. Susie, who I learned was a drama student, and I plunged headlong into a fiery relationship, fuelled by booze and drugs. We were on an emotional rollercoaster of highs and lows—mood swings that often changed several times in a single day.

Susie had been an international model for many years and had spent her time on the dark side, as many of those women do. She was very guarded about her past, but I put together a fairly accurate profile of her years as a model—then I lived with the consequences.

A few weeks into our relationship, I took her on the road. One night after a gig we were back in the Southern Cross Hotel in Melbourne, my second home from the old days, when a very strange guy continued calling our room from about 2 a.m. till dawn. He was making very improper suggestions, and despite me continually hanging up on him, he seemed determined to let me know about some shadowy liaison he'd been having with Susie for a long time. He even claimed that they were still lovers.

Susie and I were getting drunker and drunker and argumentative. When the booze made us belligerent, I picked up her bags and hurled them out the window. I immediately turned remorseful, and begged forgiveness, but by then she was out the door.

It was now 6 a.m. and the hotel guests were stirring. I charged down the hallway to the lift, naked bar a T-shirt pulled down to my knees, whimpering, but she dived into the lift with two little old ladies and left me standing there.

I pursued Susie for days on the phone, but she ignored my calls. Finally she spoke with me and said quite plainly and simply that the relationship was not going to work unless the drinking stopped.

'You're right,' I told her, and pledged my undying love. I'm fairly sure that we managed to keep on the straight and narrow for quite a while after that.

But one fateful night Susie and I were at Rod and Kathy's beautiful new house at Elizabeth Bay, right on the harbour. Rod's new pride and joy was a very expensive powerboat called a Scarab, which he'd moored right on the water in front of his house. Despite our pact, it was New Year's Eve, so we cut loose and partied into the night.

After midnight Rod took Susie and me out on the Scarab for a cruise. Rod decided it was time that I proposed to Susie. In fact he demanded that I propose to her, right there and then. But I was both drunk and stubborn, and I procrastinated.

Rod and Susie, meanwhile, took a dive into the harbour in the midnight darkness.

Finally, I somehow managed to make an impassioned proposal to Susie, who accepted. The rest of the night is a blur.

Very early on New Year's morning, Rod bundled Susie and me into his car and raced us down to an expensive jeweller in Double Bay, Sydney's most exclusive suburb. I was still wearing a terry-towelling bathrobe from the night before. Rod had called ahead and persuaded the jeweller to open his store at 8 a.m. on a public holiday. Rod and Susie disappeared inside, leaving me in a haze in the back seat.

I looked out the window and saw a woman sitting outside a coffee lounge a few doors down. I stumbled from the car in my bathrobe, and ambled up and politely asked her for a cigarette. She was an American, as I learned, on her first visit to Oz, and could barely contain her mirth. I began a bumbling explanation that I was like Australia's Brian Wilson. She burst into laughter.

'I see what you mean,' she said, lighting my cigarette, running an eye over my dishevelled state.

Susie and Rod had been inside the store for a terribly long time, so I returned to the back seat of the car. Rod finally emerged brandishing a ring, which had a price tag of $600. I thought, 'Fine, I can afford that. *Now can we go?*'

Trouble was, I hadn't asked the cost of the huge diamond that was set into the ring. When I found out, I freaked. Rod insisted that it'd be an advance against publishing royalties, and there was to be no argument about this.

Our whirlwind courtship and wedding now seems more fantasy than reality. It was decided that we should be married in a civil ceremony in Paris, with a very select group of our closest friends. So once again we flew to Europe, back to the St James Albany Hotel.

The night before the wedding, we went to see INXS play at Paris Bercy, a 25,000-seater in the heart of Paris. The band was huge in France, and the gig was a total sell-out.

Hutch sought me out, boasting that he'd bought Susie and me the biggest, whitest wedding present, and that I should immediately find Roger the bagman (their tour manager), who'd present me with Michael's gift. I found Roger, who produced a bag of ecstasy tablets. I recoiled with a mix of horror and humour—only Hutch could cook up something like this. No, no, no, I said, it was not my drug at all.

I was invited to the side of stage by the band. Chris Murphy, their manager, was also in the wings. Murphy had been so alarmed by the band's habit of excessive partying that he'd imposed a strict no-drugs policy. This was a crucial stage of INXS's career and as far as I'm aware, they'd been very well behaved.

That night Chris sent the guys out one at a time, to allow the crowd to build to fever pitch. Hutch was the last band member left side of stage. There were warm exchanges between the three of us, then, just as Michael was about to run on stage, he turned around, flashed some little white pills that he held in the palm of his hand, and threw them down his throat. Then he sprinted into the spotlight.

Murphy was furious. Sure enough, about 20 minutes into the set, the ecstasy kicked in and Michael started thrusting his groin at the audience, yelling: 'Paris—*je t'aime*. I wanna fuck ya all!'

Sidestage, I cracked up, flashing back to the Paddington Green Hotel, when they'd played for a handful of drunks.

Susie and I were married at the Australian Embassy in Paris on 30 June 1988. A small gathering of friends joined us at Hotel Ritz Paris for the reception and another night of wild partying. The INXS guys were there, as was Warners Australia boss Philip Mortlock and his wife, along with Michael Hegerty, Chippa and Hamish Cameron, who had a film crew in tow working on a documentary on INXS. Rod Muir, in typical style, ordered the very finest champagne according to our years of birth (a ceremony he later repeated with Jon Farriss). So, yes, it was a no-expense-spared evening.

We spent our wedding night in a suite at Hotel Ritz and then set out on our honeymoon around Europe. We headed south to Florence, but really had no schedule, no clear plan. We just jumped in the car and let the wind take us wherever it blew. We first drove all over the South of France, and when we felt tired, we just checked into anywhere that looked appealing. If we were hungry, we found somewhere and ate. We were totally free, not shackled to any kind of schedule or itinerary.

The trip took us all over northern Italy, up through Monaco and Switzerland to Germany. I took Susie to meet Volker and Andrea, but unfortunately Volker and Susie took an instant dislike to each other, and Susie behaved rather badly and I thought very rudely to my old friend. It's not the first time: for some odd reason, while I've always had the best relationships with my German friends, my Australian friends have trouble assimilating into their culture.

25

'i knew i'd never be a king, but don't you take away my dreams'

Here inside of Me

Back in Oz, despite my protestations, Rod insisted we hold a second wedding reception at Sydney's Sebel Townhouse. This was going to be a very lavish affair with a huge number of guests and a very impressive celebrity list; it was really a PR exercise to get my profile up for the *Glory Road* album.

These lavish weddings sure take up an enormous amount of time, money and effort, and I wasn't at all comfortable. Jimmy Barnes sang a great version of 'When a Man Loves a Woman', while I danced uncomfortably with Susie; I always was a lousy dancer. The reception itself was quite stellar at first, yet veered down the path of pure decadence as the night rolled on.

After midnight, it became more like a night at Benny's than a wedding party. However, we did get our fair share of publicity so I guess the night achieved its purpose. Because Susie had an excellent relationship with her agent, Peter Chadwick, and I had a PR machine going on around me, we became A-list celebrities for some time afterwards. Still, I found (and still find) fame an uncomfortable and undesirable way to live my life. It takes up so much oxygen that there's little time left for doing anything worthwhile, like writing songs. Kids can have their 15 minutes of fame—it's not for me.

❖

I put together another great band and we set off on what was to be a long and arduous tour. It became another instance where everything started to go a little crazy after months on the road. I was only being paid a wage of $340 a week by MMA—INXS's management company, who were managing me—whereas the band were on a weekly wage of $1500 each. It's probably just as well; the entourage was partying hard every night and it was better that I was always short of money, otherwise I could have spiralled right out of control. A couple of the band members had sex worker girlfriends who were bringing drugs to the band in every corner of Australia. There had been decadent Richard Clapton Bands in the past, but these guys were the champions of partying.

The workload was a killer, and the obligatory partying every night started really taking its toll. We somehow managed to perform well, but I was burnt out after a relatively short time. I just didn't feel like we were achieving anything, except maybe wrecking our health. I soon began to feel that it just wasn't worth it.

Rod Muir spoke with me; he was very critical of the way the tour was going, and finally decided that he would sack the management. This, of course, was an enormous drama, but Rod was still my mentor, someone who'd made a fairly serious investment in my career, and he decided to pull the plug. I was a wreck and people were starting to talk.

So we came off the road, and Rod decided that I should go and work for him in his office. This, in principle, seemed a most sensible (if unlikely) idea. It would give me time to consider my next move. However, the plan backfired, as Rod and I slipped back into our old habits. There was French champagne on tap and I was arriving home to Susie every night in an inebriated state.

Then Susie had news: she was pregnant (although this pregnancy didn't go the distance). She put her foot down—and savagely. She gave me an ultimatum as she was driving me to Rod's office one day. In heavy traffic, she jammed her foot on the brakes, and demanded I get out of the car.

'It's me or Rod!' Susie said.

Since she was going to be the mother of our children it was a bit of a no brainer, and I complied. My fantasy world with Rod came to an abrupt end.

Susie and I moved into a rented flat in Bellevue Hill just a few minutes' walk from Triple M, Sydney's vanguard radio station. It was still OK for me to hang out with the people there, just not get crazy with the boss. Triple M was the most fun place to be, and I was a frequent visitor. I'd befriended huge-rating DJ Doug Mulray and his celebrated team, which included Andrew Denton and Dave Gibson (he of a thousand voices). I guess I sort of became the station mascot. I also formed lasting friendships with the stars like Jono and Danno, Rob Duckworth and Stuart Cranney and the Club Veg guys, as well as the folks in the back room, people like Trevor and Jan Smith, Charlie Fox and Hamish (Hulk) Cameron, the producers and directors.

It was a marvellous, tight-knit family. My socialising invariably led to me appearing on air. I became part of this crazy crew, who breathed so much fun and life and music into this town.

Australian broadcasting was at its peak in the eighties. In my view, broadcasters like Triple M were an important part of the character and fabric of Sydney. All the shenanigans that went on made for a rich tapestry of life outside the 9 to 5 grind, providing relief from the dull grey existence that pervaded the lives of normal people. Life was lived in the fast lane, and the Cross, Benny's, Springfields and the Manzil Room were the modern-day speakeasies, places where everyone congregated until dawn.

Of course, drugs were everywhere. Drug-taking within media circles was widespread. I find it amusing to watch, read and listen to the exact same former fast-living journos, radio stars and TV personalities now pontificating about the evils of drugs. It really is quite sad that the 'no-fun zone' of the new millennium has sapped the very essence out of life in Australia, so now people are only free to work, eat, sleep and pay taxes and bills. I firmly believe in a God, but I'm sure he didn't intend us to be wasting our lives on this mind-numbingly depressing existence.

I have a theory that when Rod Muir left Australian radio in the late 1980s, the entire country began to shift to the right. Music became corporatised, and multinational companies, intent on profit rather than on fostering original talent, signed up acts that catered for the majority taste. It was the beginning of the end.

So I really treasure the last couple of years of my personal rollercoaster ride. In my case it was probably just as well I eventually slowed down, because I was playing with a band of bad boys, still living life as if there was no tomorrow. After the *Glory Road* era, I had to think about doing something more constructive with my life.

Philip Mortlock suggested we produce a live album, but not merely another contract-fulfilling live set. This would be one of the classiest live albums ever produced in this country. I assembled a stellar group of musicians, people I knew well, like Jimmy Barnes, Jon Farriss and Garry Gary Beers, along with Venetta Fields, plus Michael Hegerty and Kirk Lorange from the *Goodbye Tiger* days. The record company constructed a small sound stage in Sydney's Artarmon where we'd record the best songs of my career, live before an invited audience, on 16 April 1989.

We rehearsed for a number of days on a roster system, but the guitar player demanded an outrageous fee, and was promptly dumped. In a panic I employed a very young guitarist, Ben Butler, the son of a federal senator and the Australian Ambassador to the United Nations, and threw him in at the deep end. I took Ben into the rehearsal room and introduced him to the all-star band.

'Oh,' I said to Ben, 'we'll be recording the gig tonight.'

Ben's playing was nothing short of spectacular, and can still be heard on the album, which was aptly titled *The Best Years of Our Lives*.

Despite the absence of drugs, some imbibing took place under the radar. The concert was recorded in four parts, and during the third quarter, just as the director counted us in, a techie in the recording truck nodded off, slumping onto the console, totally catatonic. His quick-thinking assistant whacked him over the head and hit the red record button, missing only the first three beats of Jonnie Farriss's drum intro.

In the break before the last quarter I was busting for a piss, and the irate director told me to slip into a tiny room behind the stage and piss in the sink.

'And be back in 30 seconds!'

I ducked into the darkened room, attended to business and jumped back on stage. I introduced 'I Am an Island', the last song of the night, and as I was talking, Jimmy came hurtling out onto the stage growling: 'You fucking music industry wankers, you're as boring as batshit! Get up off your fucking arses.' Then he hurled himself on to the front table and sent champagne bottles and glasses flying everywhere, yelling: 'I'm gonna kick your fucking arses to fucking death!' But Jimmy was laughing his guts out throughout this mayhem, so it was patently obvious that this was just one of Barnesy's practical jokes.

We had only a few days to mix the entire concert, ready to be aired on prime time on Channel Ten the following Friday night. We mixed and mixed with barely any sleep, triumphantly delivering the master tapes to Warners on the Friday morning. I was utterly exhausted and not even sure I would be able to stay up until 8.30 to watch the concert on TV.

But during the afternoon, all hell broke loose. Normally, a TV network would not bother auditioning a show like this before they put it to air. However, I had enthusiastic fans at Channel Ten who'd decided to give themselves a sneak preview. The boss of the network phoned Philip Mortlock, outraged and threatening to pull the show off air. We had been so exhausted at the end of the mixing we had left in the Jimmy Barnes bit, about 'kick your fucking arses to fucking death!' Peace was made, his outburst was edited, and the show made it on air.

Shortly afterwards, Jon Farriss invited Susie and me up to his apartment at Stanley, in Hong Kong. He and Michael Hutchence had relocated there, but Michael was in a whirlwind relationship with Kylie Minogue, and they were jet-setting around the world. Jon had the place to himself. Their apartment was stunning, just beautiful. The vista from the windows reminded me of Monte Carlo, and the houses in the area were unbelievable.

Jonnie and I planned to do as much songwriting as possible during my stay and initially we churned them out. I wrote 'Happy Valley', which appeared on my *Distant Thunder* album, and it still reminds me of those carefree days in Honkers.

The record company had decided we should shoot a video for 'Ace of Hearts' in Hong Kong, so Philip Mortlock flew up Phil Deamer, who'd produced the video for 'Angelou' a couple of years earlier. Phil decided that we should employ a model to play my girlfriend and we were like kids in a candy store, thumbing through the photos of all the local models. We decided on a Colombian girl, Vivien, because of her fiery good looks—and her acting ability, of course. She proved to be an excellent choice.

Phil's choice for the other guy in the story was a gallant Frenchman, a local nightclub identity. The rest of the crew was Chinese. The entire video was great fun. For three days we drove through every little nook and cranny of Hong Kong, including the New Territories, which are extraordinarily beautiful, dotted with ancient villages that must have been unoccupied for who knows how long; the tranquillity around the various waterways was so cathartic. I couldn't think of a better way to experience Hong Kong.

On the last night of the shoot, Phil directed Vivien and me acting out a vicious lover's tiff on a busy Hong Kong street. Apparently we acted it out a bit too well. For a long time afterwards I had trouble convincing Susie that there'd been nothing going on between Vivien and myself. Susie refused to believe that I could act that well.

In the last scene of the video, we took the crew up to Vivien's apartment, about forty floors up. Then Phil wanted to film a rather juicy scene between Vivien and myself. When we learnt that her boyfriend—an Italian New Yorker—was due home at any moment, I leaned over the balcony and freaked. I don't think we actually went ahead with the scene.

I stayed on for a further few weeks, writing more with Jon. There was so much chatter from all the band members, who were scattered all over the globe. One morning I woke up hours before Jonnie and the fax machine was spewing out an incredibly long document. It took me ages to recognise that it was a six-foot-long drawing of a penis, courtesy of Tim Farriss. At least the guys still had their sense of humour.

But I knew it was time to get back to Australia. Soon after my return, Susie became pregnant with our first-born. I find it amusing that our children were conceived in Michael's bedroom in Hong Kong, so there's a claim to fame.

I was back on the road, about to go onstage at The Arts Factory in Byron Bay, when I received an urgent phone call from Susie. I was really worried that something might be wrong, but she told me something completely unexpected.

'We're having twins,' she told me.

For the initial few months of the pregnancy, Saskia and Montana, our daughters, had been right on top of each other in the womb; the ultrasounds had revealed what we thought was one rather large baby. Now there were two.

I was relieved and deliriously happy.

You don't know what you've got til it's gone

When I finally completed writing this bunch of memoirs documenting my experiences from the late sixties to 1990, I was anxious to have my daughters sanction my work. Obviously, I was worried about the tales from the dark side and did not want to publish a book that would in any way embarrass them. Their response was really interesting. They brushed aside the references to all the partying, metaphorically patted me on the head, and told me that they had always known about my wild ways back in the day. Their reactions to my shenanigans were nonchalant to say the least.

Despite it all, my girls have grown to be well-adjusted young adults. They are simply my *raison d'être*. The fact that they are identical twins is an added blessing, because they are like bookends.

Saskia is a music obsessive; she grew out of nineties pop very quickly and, by the time she was in her late teens, she was listening to Etta James and Otis Rush and the purest of blues artists. She is now 'teaching' me about Talking Heads and Richard Thompson. Isn't that ironic?

Montana, on the other hand, went on to study Japanese at Sydney University. She now lives in Tokyo and has introduced me to Hikaru Utada and some of the better J Pop acts. Montana was a gifted drummer at an early age, but gave it away after a few years. It's her life and she deserves her own space, and I totally respect the choices she has made. You see what I mean about bookends? One of my daughters is an obsessive musician who is into Talking Heads and the other is into J Pop and living in Tokyo!

But it was my documenting of a golden age that was of most significance to my daughters. And they asked: 'What the hell happened to the world?'

To so many young people, the Old World is a world of wonder—a vibrant, colourful and exciting time that has now been replaced by a world more akin to George Orwell's *1984*. We are now just white rats on treadmills forced to do our master's bidding, which is simply work work work and more work. I am well aware that the phrase 'panacea of the masses' belongs to a political and theological argument, but one could just as easily apply it to what is happening to our lives today. The evening news is a smokescreen, ignoring real information and keeping the realities of life hidden behind bright, shiny illusions: Kim Kardashian's ingrown toenail, or Miley Cyrus coming down with the flu because she has been gallivanting around buck naked for too long. This is the stuff that now dominates the news and totally eclipses what is really going on.

The arch larrikins I remember from my childhood—such as Bea Miles, Frank Thring and a long list of notable characters—have long passed on, with no eccentrics left to colour our world. Let's face it, we live in a 'no-fun zone' and are so trapped by political correctness that we have forgotten how to live. As Basil Fawlty said: '. . . that particular avenue of pleasure has been closed off!'

When I reminisce about the last 25 years, it is easy to see the progress of the seismic shift that has brought us to this point. I'll make music the centrepiece of all this because, after all, that is what I know best. However, there are much broader ramifications.

I reckon that way back in the day—the late sixties—the conservatives eyed off the anarchistic young rockers with utter contempt and fear. But then the most successful bands of the day slowly moved out of the garage and eventually ended up filling stadiums. At this point the corporations noticed the music industry growing exponentially into a business worth billions. I believe that the corporations then became determined to grab a piece of this action for themselves.

YOU DON'T KNOW WHAT YOU'VE GOT TIL IT'S GONE

By the time I entered the music industry, record companies were already noticeably influenced by their accountants. The accountants were representing the interests of the corporations (who now owned the record companies), and the pursuit of profits started to overtake and ultimately eclipse the purity of music as an art. As I said early on in this book, I initially found this abhorrent, and kicked hard against the pricks, making life difficult for myself in my early years as a musician.

I kept running back to Berlin, chasing a cultural world that was fading fast, until Volker finally convinced me that I could perhaps still manage to survive in the music industry with a little 'rat-cunning'. So I wrote 'Girls on the Avenue', appeared on *Countdown* and played the corporate game, and I have managed to survive in this business for 40 years. But despite my difficult beginnings, I would have to say that this has been one fantastic ride and I wouldn't swap it for anything. Sure, a lot of things have pissed me off, but over this 40-year rollercoaster ride, the good times have certainly outweighed the bad.

However, having said that, the problem for my generation is that the music of the last ten years or so has become so heavily marketed that it is about as exciting as shrink-wrapped products on a supermarket shelf. Many modern songs are egocentric and self-obsessed, and they are pretty silly when one considers the relatively limited lives and experience of the writers. Most of the time, the 'angst' described by some young writers is just a bit supercilious. One wonders how much they have really experienced. I don't mean the trials of adolescence that we all experience—I mean real angst. The problem with the 'Me' generation of pop stars is that they simply don't seem to have done much of anything, so there is not much to mesmerise the public. There are no stories to tell, no real adventures; ostensibly they have led quite sheltered lives and seem solely motivated by the desire to make a lot of money. So they study commerce and marketing and this becomes a prerequisite for a career in music. (Yes, this may be a sweeping generalisation, but more often than not this is the way things are nowadays.)

For about the past 20 years, music has lapsed into a homogenised and rather uninteresting state, because the system that dictates what we will and won't hear is based on false principles. Pop music is fine unless it is taken too seriously, but it is about as satisfying as a Big Mac. It's okay while you're eating it, but has no lasting nutritional value and therefore is ultimately unsatisfying, and you feel like shit afterwards. This probably explains why many reunion tours by pop stars of the past fail.

As a musician, I need the challenge and stimulation of my peer group pushing the envelope and coming from left of centre with bold new ideas that challenge the boundaries of music. Otherwise, the music becomes stale and homogenised and is just not fun anymore. I will always remember hearing the first album by the British band The The in London in the early eighties, and thinking to myself that music had reached a brave new frontier, that there would be truly interesting and exciting times ahead. There were a number of acts around in the early eighties who showed promise of a real New Wave (as opposed to the heavily marketed 'hairdresser bands' who bastardised the term). There were cool things happening with World Music (Mory Kante) and Kraut Rock (Kraftwerk) and, more significantly, some of the post-punk bands were trying different and interesting ideas (The Blue Nile, Talking Heads). Yet, somehow, most of this music has failed to survive the test of time (not Talking Heads, of course), and I suspect that this is a result of the dumbing down of music.

My generation grew up with bona fide iconic heroes who were, in every way, 'the real shit'. The music of the new millennium too often fails in the most vacuous way, because it is simply an imitation of the real thing. As a reaction to this many young people I know are going back and listening to old albums that were recorded 40 or 50 years ago. In recent years, a career in music has often been contemptuously treated as merely a vehicle for becoming rich and famous in the quickest possible time and by the easiest route.

Many of the young people on today's talent shows appear to be experts at the art of mimicry. Fifty years ago our parents would buy us those 'paint-by-numbers' kits, where all we had to do was make sure we painted neatly and tidily between the lines of a Mona Lisa outline, and the end result was quite impressive. But that didn't turn a kid into Leonardo da Vinci! Too often I get the feeling that a lot of the apparently talented kids nowadays are more akin to a building façade on a set at Universal City. There just doesn't feel like there's a lot going on—'light's on, but nobody home!'

Then again, the more I heard about the angst-ridden alternative bands of the 1990s, the more I learnt that in private life many of these stars were merely young capitalists who had found an easy way to accumulate vast wealth—simply by masquerading in ripped jeans and flannel shirts. (The tour manager of one of the world's biggest alternative bands told me that as soon as they came off tour their whole persona morphed into attire and behaviour that was more akin to bankers and stockbrokers than rebellious rock stars. Oh, I see—so it was just an 'act'.)

In this new millennium, I guess one would have to credit aspiring pop stars with being a bit more honest than their 'indie' predecessors. Today, young artists quite plainly state in interviews that their priorities for a career in music are to find the right stylist and personal trainer, followed by the right lawyer and accountant before they go chasing a record deal.

Jack Black's *School of Rock* was packed full of gems like:

'There used to be a way to stick it to the Man. It was called rock'n'roll!'

'Rock is about passion, man. Where's the joy?'

'You forgot about one thing. It's called music!'

YOU DON'T KNOW WHAT YOU'VE GOT TIL IT'S GONE

Let's face it. So much of modern music is just a sign of the times. Too often it is dull and colourless, just like the world it is reflecting. Many of the current crop of modern musicians don't seem interested in their listeners; and more often than not their music is simply myopic. Instead of music being a vital and integral part of people's (the listeners') lives, it has become disconnected and egocentric.

Something else that I feel has been badly overlooked is the *perfect imperfection* that once gave rock music its soul and *joie de vivre*. Nowadays music is made on computers. The timing is locked into a grid, the pitch is corrected by 'auto tune' and hit songs can be written to a blueprint or template. As a consequence, the rhythm has lost its swing and those delicious blue notes by singers of the past (especially the blues singers) have been overcorrected so that the vocals lack soul; in reality it is actually the computers making the music. Modern music software is absolutely incredible—but it is vitally important that the musician *uses the computer* instead of allowing the computer to rule them and produce the music by machine.

To make matters worse, it seems that whenever really worthwhile young artists manage to scratch and claw their way to the middle, they are given their fifteen minutes of fame and disappear as quickly as they appeared in the first place. My iTunes library is littered with lots of these young artists, many of whom are really talented, but simply can't get any traction. Maybe this is because the only successful music artists nowadays are so corporatised that their music is little more than an advertising jingle.

So you may wonder whether there are any younger artists that I actually do like—a lot. Yeah. Ryan Adams. A truly great songwriter in the accepted sense of 'great'. Jack White—he is really cool!! Used to love Frou Frou (speaking of pop music) but they made one brilliant album then Imogen Heap drifted off somewhere. But then there are the Foo Fighters, Wilco, Black Rebel Motorcycle Club, Robert Glasper, Laura Mvula, etc etc etc. There have been a lot of other artists who showed much promise before they disappeared into the ether. Maybe this is because there is simply too much music. There are so many aspiring young music acts these days, one wonders if there are more music acts than there are people available to listen to them. (There was a very interesting and thought-provoking article titled 'The Long Tail', published in *Wired Magazine* in 2004, which you may be interested to read.)

Nevertheless, I would like to believe that we can still turn this thing around. Music is a vital part of the human condition. It serves as a catharsis we cannot live without, and it should just make us feel good within ourselves, with our fellow man and the world in which we live. I love the huge sign on the side of the Tower Records building in Tokyo: 'NO MUSIC, NO LIFE'!

Thank God, life is cyclical. There is no way I would want to be seen as simply a grumpy old man, raving and ranting about 'back in my day, son'. Back in my day, life could be pretty bloody awful, too. Back in my day, we watched in horror as the Bay of Pigs incident unfurled; we had Pat Boone on the radio and we lived on a diet of Chiko Rolls. So no—I am not singing the praises of 'my day!'

If you refer back to the early chapters of this book, you will see that I was born into a world of McCarthyism and Menzies, of a steel-fisted Christian Coalition which turned us against each other and was largely responsible for the savage rampant violence on the streets of Sydney in the sixties. Young people were oppressed and full of pent-up but misguided energy and rage. Not just in Sydney but in London and Brighton and elsewhere in the world. Yet, somehow, the hippies managed to turn this around so absolutely, but not without great sacrifice. It took years and years of marching in the streets, sometimes resulting in loss of lives; the Stones wrote 'Street Fighting Man' as an anthem for the times. Although it's an awful cliché, 'no pain—no gain' rings so true. The myopic egocentricity that is now so prevalent impedes our everyday lives so much, and without realising it, we surrender to the faceless one per cent who control most of the world's wealth and therefore keep us being the white rats on the treadmill. So while we are totally distracted watching gorgeous young chicky babes getting their gear off on MTV, the capitalists are tightening the screws. (This is the bright, shiny end of the long tail.)

The music of the 1950s and early 1960s, epitomised by Annette Funicello, Frankie Avalon and the Mickey Mouse

Club, was just a vacuous waste of vinyl. And I'm talking about way before *American Idol*. Yet somehow, in the fifties, a small group of musicians (both black and white) with real integrity managed to survive, despite having to endure great hardship. From those little embryos of music emerged the Beatles and the Stones, and a gigantic cultural movement was born.

I am immensely proud of the fact that I was able to be part of the beginnings of a revolution in Australian Rock. We endured considerable hardship (I couldn't even pay the rent in my first twelve years as a professional musician). My posse of musical mates just lived to play real music without any regard for whether it would lead to a profitable career or not. And so, from acts such as Chisel and The Oils and then INXS was born 'Oz Rock'.

On a personal level, the last 25 years have been a lot of fun. Just different, that's all. I truly believe that *Diamond Mine* and *Harlequin Nights* are by far my best albums, and I'd like to think I finally figured out how to craft great songs. But you get that. Every artist is going to dote on their newest songs, for fairly obvious reasons.

Quite frankly, I used to view some of my earlier songs like 'Deep Water' as a bit amateurish and ramshackle, and it used to frustrate the hell out of me that some of my more recent songs were unfairly ignored. But John Lennon said something back in the day like, although songs are like children to the writer, once we put them out there in the public domain they then belong to the listener. At that point it is not up to the writer to be the judge of his or her own work. These days I try to show respect for some of my earlier songs because you love them, and that is simply how it is. You have all given me so much for so many years and I have sacrosanct respect for that.

Seven years ago I was coerced into attempting a solo gig at Sydney's magnificent State Theatre. As daunting as that was, I jumped in at the deep end and to my surprise we had a hit. In the second year the first show sold out in less than an hour and we went into a second show. This tradition has endured for several years now despite the fact that none of us has really understood the serendipity of its continued success. My theory is that it has much to do with the State Theatre itself. There just seems to be something about Richard Clapton at the State Theatre that resonates with people. It could be that people who want to see a Richard Clapton gig do not want to stand on a beer-soaked carpet in a pub. But then again there could be a lot more to it than that.

So. Forty years, eh? Before I know it, I'll be hurtling into my 41st year as a musician. Believe it or not, I seem to become more and more passionate about music as the years go on. There are always going to be more songs to write—I'm not sure I've hit my peak yet. And there is no greater pleasure than going out with the band and playing more gigs. Maybe there will be a lot more stories to tell about the years since 1990 and beyond. 'Bop till you drop!' That's what I reckon.

I'd like to think that this book is as much about you as it is about me and that's why, as predictable as the title may seem, it had to be called *The Best Years of Our Lives*.

Discography

Prussian Blue

1973, Festival Records

Produced and engineered by Richard Batchens at Festival Studios

Hardly Know Myself / Southern Germany / Poor Man's Saviour / Strange Days in Chippendale / Prussian Blue / I Wanna Be a Survivor / Last Train to Marseilles / All the Prodigal Children / Burning Ships / The Lonesome Voyager

Girls on the Avenue

1975, Festival Records

Produced and engineered by Richard Batchens at Festival Studios

Girls on the Avenue / Down the Road / Blue Bay Blues / Throw Me Down a Line / Burn Down Your Bridges / Rose Wine Café / Ode to a Slow Boat / I Fell for You / The Ride Out

Mainstreet Jive

1976, Festival Records

Produced and engineered by Richard Batchens at Festival Studios

Soldier of Fortune / Suit Yourself / Kickin' the Moon Around /

Lonesome Heart / Need a Visionary / Factory Life / Casanova's Got the Blues / Islands of the Heart

Highway One
1976, Festival Records
Produced and engineered by Richard Batchens at Festival Studios

Capricorn Dancer / Babe Rainbow / Down the Road / Longshore Rider / Highway One / Highway One #2

Goodbye Tiger
1977, Festival Records
Produced by Richard Batchens / Engineered by John Frolich at Festival Studios

Lucky Country / Wild Child / Goodbye Tiger / I Can Talk to You / Deep Water / Out on the Edge Again / Hiding From the Light / Amsterdam

Past Hits and Previews
1978, Festival Records
Remastered by Joe Hansch at Kendun Recorders, Los Angeles

Stepping Across the Line / When the Heat's Off plus hits from previous albums

DISCOGRAPHY

Hearts on the Nightline
1979, Festival Records
Produced by Dallas Smith / Engineered by Alex Vertikoff at Soundcastle Studios, Los Angeles

Hearts on the Nightline / Passing Trains / Ace of Hearts / Down the Tracks / Sometimes the Fire / Mainstreet Hustle / Out on the Island / Throw Me Down a Line / Thorn in My Saddle

Dark Spaces
1980, Festival Records
Produced by Richard Clapton / Engineered by Mark Moffat at Festival Studios

I Just Can't Make It / High Society / Shadows / Sophisticated Girl / Dark Spaces / Get Back to the Shelter / Le Club des Fools / The Working Class Life / Metropolis

The Great Escape
1982, WEA Records
Produced by Mark Opitz / Engineered by Mark Opitz and Dave Walsh at Paradise Studios, Sydney

I Am an Island / The Universal / Spellbound / Flow in Motion / The Best Years of Our Lives / Syncopation Train / I Fought the Law / All Night Long / Walk on Water

Solidarity

1984, Mushroom Records

Produced by Mark Opitz / Engineered by David Nicholas at Rhinoceros Studios, Sydney

The Heart of It / Chinatown (Richard Clapton/Tony Slavich) / Amsterdam / Kathleen (Richard Clapton/Guy Delandro) / Solidarity / Feelin' Alright Tonight / Katy's Leaving Babylon / Cry Mercy Sister / Atom Bomb / New World

Glory Road

1987, WEA Records

Produced by Jon Farriss / Engineered by David Nicholas at Rhinoceros Studios, Sydney, and Studios de la Grande Armée, Paris / Mixed by Chris Lord-Alge at The Hit Factory, New York

Trust Somebody / The Night Train / Glory Road / I Didn't Wanna Make You Stay / Emperor's New Clothes (Richard Clapton/Jon Farriss/Tim Farriss/Garry Gary Beers) / Chameleons (Richard Clapton/Jimmy Barnes/Jon Farriss) / The Underground (Jon Farriss/Richard Clapton) / Down to the Ark / Angelou / Modern Life

The Best Years of Our Lives

1989, WEA Records

Recorded by Al Wright at One Zero One, Sydney / Mixed by Al

DISCOGRAPHY

Wright, Richard Clapton and Mark Bergin at Apocalypse Studios, Crow's Nest

Deep Water / Trust Somebody / Ace of Hearts / Blue Bay Blues / Get Back to the Shelter / The Night Train / Capricorn Dancer / Lucky Country / High Society / Girls on the Avenue / Goodbye Tiger / Angelou / Glory Road / I Am an Island / The Best Years of Our Lives

Distant Thunder
1993, Sony Music/Columbia
Produced by Richard Clapton / Engineered by Niven Garland at Rhinoceros Studios, Sydney

Distant Thunder / Oceans of the Heart / All Fall Down (Richard Clapton/John McKay) / Happy Valley (Jon Farriss/Richard Clapton) / Don't Be a Stranger / Here Inside of Me / Up Where the Angels Fly / Precious / Stop Foolin' Around (Richard Clapton/Jon Farriss) / Real Love (Richard Clapton/John McKay)

Angeltown
1996, Gypsy Music/Village Roadshow
Produced by Richard Clapton / Engineered by Richard Clapton at Mudgeeraba, Garry Gary Beers' home studio/ Mixed by David Nicholas at Eclipse Studios, Sydney

Dixieland / My Mind's Eye / That Moon (Diesel/Richard Clapton) / Stay With Me / Howl (Sam McNally/Richard Clapton) / I Wish I Was in Paris / Turn My Heart Around (Richard Clapton/Diesel) / Shine a Light / The Devil in Paradise / Angeltown (Richard Clapton/Dave Leslie) / Real Life (is stranger than fiction)

The Definitive Anthology
1999, WEA Records

Girls on the Avenue / Capricorn Dancer / Lucky Country / Deep Water / Goodbye Tiger / Get Back to the Shelter / I Am an Island / The Best Years of Our Lives / Solidarity / Trust Somebody / Glory Road / Ace of Hearts / Distant Thunder / Oceans of the Heart / Calling for You (Richard Clapton/Tim Farriss/Guy Delandro) / Little Pilgrims / Blue Bay Blues / The Universal / Walk on Water / Angelou / Real Love / Love Is Strong (Richard Clapton/Michael Hegerty/Mark Edwards) / Everybody's Makin' Money (Except Me)

Up and Down the Glory Road
2001, WEA Records

Lucky Country / Capricorn Dancer / Suit Yourself / Get Back to the Shelter / Real Love / Dark Spaces / Oceans of the Heart / Spellbound / Calling For You (Richard Clapton/Tim Farriss/

DISCOGRAPHY

Guy Delandro) / Distant Thunder / Deep Water / That Moon (Diesel/Richard Clapton) / The Underground (Jon Farriss/Richard Clapton) / Glory Road / Ace of Hearts / Flow in Motion / I Am an Island / The Best Years of Our Lives / Girls on the Avenue / Blue Bay Blues / Goodbye Tiger

Diamond Mine

2004, Warner Music

Produced by Richard Clapton / Mixed by Rick Will at Studios 301, Sydney

Obsession (Richard Clapton/Guy Delandro) / Some Sunny Day / Bomb the Bomb / Diamond Mine / High as the Heavens / The Simple Things / Head Full of Rain / Paradise Drive / Zweite Neon / The Dark End of the Road / Tides of Time / What Does It Take to Get Lucky / All Stand Together

Rewired

2006, Warner Music

Produced by Richard Clapton

Trust Somebody / Blue Bay Blues / Liberty Bell / Glory Road / Get Back to the Shelter / Goodbye Tiger / Up Where the Angels Fly / Katy's Leaving Babylon / High Society / Hearts on the Nightline / Capricorn Dancer / Prussian Blue / Ace of Hearts

Harlequin Nights

2012, MGM

Produced by Richard Clapton / Mixed by David Nicholas

Sunny Side Up / Vapour Trails / Blue Skies / Run Like a River / Dancing with the Vampires / Over the Borderline / Blowing Smoke Up at the Moon / One Fine Day / Skanky Town / Shady Love / Keep Your Blue Eyes Open Wide

For more details of compilations and anthologies, go to www.richardclapton.com

Index of songs

Ace of Hearts, 176, 183, 313
Amsterdam, 233, 235
Angelou, 274, 284, 313
Atom Bomb, 232
Best Years of Our Lives, The, 199, 216–17
Blue Bay Blues, 91
Burning Ships, 66
Capricorn Dancer, 126, 131, 139, 142, 143, 166
Cry Mercy Sister, 235
Dark Spaces, 188
Deep Water, 125, 129, 138, 139, 141, 326
Emperor's New Clothes, 281
Everybody's Making Money (Except Me), 186
Factory Life, 68
Feelin' Alright Tonight, 236
Flow in Motion, 200
Girls on the Avenue, 87, 95, 96, 97, 98, 102, 116, 319
Glory Road, 253, 282, 289, 296
Goodbye Barbara-Ann, 251–2
Goodbye Tiger, 128, 151–2, 214
Happy Valley, 313
Heart of It, The, 236

I Am an Island, 199, 201, 210, 240, 265, 312
I Can Talk to You, 140
I Fought the Law, 201
I Wanna Be a Survivor, 86
Kathleen, 234
Katy's Leaving Babylon, 232
Kickin' the Moon Around, 108
Last Train to Marseilles, 86, 87, 90
Lucky Country, 129, 141
Need a Visionary, 108
New World, 233
Poor Man's Saviour, 55, 68
Prussian Blue, 66, 131
Solidarity, 233
Southern Germany, 55
Stepping Across the Line, 161
Suit Yourself, 108, 118, 162
Transpac Slide, The, 272
Travelling Down the Castlereagh, 97, 98
Trust Somebody, 281
Under the Knife, 276
Underground, The, 275
Universal, The, 200, 201

RICHARD CLAPTON
BEST YEARS 1974–2014
THE 40TH ANNIVERSARY COLLECTION

A brand-new and definitive career-spanning four-disc set. Includes all the hits and fan favourites plus rarities across three CDs, together with, for the first time ever on DVD, the classic 1988 concert film *The Best Years of Our Lives*, featuring performances from Jimmy Barnes, Venetta Fields, Kirk Lorange, Michael Hegerty, Garry Gary Beers, Jon Farriss and others. Features deluxe packaging and includes liner notes by Toby Creswell and David Pepperell as well as numerous previously unseen images.

www.richardclapton.com
www.warnermusic.com.au
www.facebook.com/YourOldStuff